Sounding Forth the Trumpet
for Children

Sounding Forth the Trumpet for Children

Peter Marshall and David Manuel
with Anna Wilson Fishel

Revell

a division of Baker Publishing Group
Grand Rapids, Michigan

THE DIVINE WATCHMAKER

The LORD looks from heaven;
He sees all the sons of men;
From His dwelling place He looks out
On all the inhabitants of the earth. (Psalm 33:13–14)

Imagine that God has invited you to peer inside a huge, gold pocket watch stretched across the night sky. The watch is filled with sparkling wheels and gears of all shapes and sizes. At first you see the glistening mainspring, so big it doesn't seem to move at all. Then you spot the smaller parts, ticking in timed measurements.

When you look more closely, you detect a few bright gears meshing together so other gears and wheels can turn. You also notice those which only seem to turn themselves. You marvel at the delicate and precise movements. The Watchmaker who built this system must be very intelligent, you think. Only He knows the role assigned to each individual wheel and each separate part. And only He understands that what appears to be a little cog in this great big watch can be that very part responsible for the chiming of the hour.

The story of the years before the Civil War is a story much like this enormous pocket watch. We can look at many of the events. We can read about the people and watch the hands of

Slavery is the practice of owning another person as property. After Eli Whitney's invention of the cotton gin in 1793, the growing of cotton exploded in the South. One machine could separate cotton from its seed in the same time it had taken 50 people before. The Southern soil and climate created a perfect cotton-growing environment. The South needed laborers and lots of them. Slavery already existed, so all a farmer had to do was buy a few slaves and begin or expand his business. By the time war broke out in 1861, nearly 4 million slaves lived in the United States.

God's Plan

America was to be one nation—under God. And as all men are equal before God, each citizen was to be equal to any other. From the beginning, the Pilgrims and Puritans had tried to live this vision. Our forefathers wrote it into the Declaration of Independence:

> . . . that all men are created equal,
> that they are endowed by their Creator
> with certain unalienable Rights,
> that among these are Life, Liberty
> and the pursuit of Happiness.

They documented it in the Constitution by creating a government that recognized these rights. They fought and died for it.

But how can one person own another and yet the two be equal? This was the heart of the slavery question. Many people believed slavery was wrong. The problem was, no one knew what to do about it. If the government freed the slaves, where would they go and what would they do? How would slave owners be paid for their losses? The government didn't have enough money to buy all the slaves. The framers of the Constitution found no solution, so they left the slavery issue alone.

In 1820 the question of admitting Missouri as a slave state stirred up such a hornet's nest that John Quincy Adams wrote, "a dissolution . . . of the Union could certainly be necessary." Congress however, was able to frame a compromise: Any state admitted below latitude 36° 30′ (Missouri's southern border) would be a slave state and any state coming in above it would be free. The government breathed a sigh of relief, and everyone hoped the problem would go away.

But it couldn't, and it didn't. Why? Because God's call to become one nation under Him had not changed. While equality might have been just words on parchment paper during the early 1800s, it was still His spiritual truth and it had to be worked into a living reality in everyone's heart.

This book presents the story of the years before war broke out between the North and the South, before 1861. As you read, you'll discover some people who understood God's plan and moved in it. You'll find others who did not. You'll also meet those who risked their lives to bring God's plan about. You'll be amazed as the right man or woman shows up in the right place at the right time. And you'll observe the Watchmaker so precisely adjust the timing of the wheels and gears of events that everything falls into place like clockwork.

How did the Lord do it? Whom did He use? Get ready to come along and find out as this book continues the exciting story of America's struggle to become one nation under God.

As he scanned it, the Congressman frowned slightly. While the petition appeared genuine, Adams instantly realized something was wrong.

"Sir," he hesitated, "I believe I should ask you for a decision on this one. It purports to be from 22 persons declaring themselves to be slaves."

The Congressional chamber exploded. Immediately, Southern representatives from Alabama, Virginia, Georgia, and the Carolinas jumped to their feet.

"The gentleman from Massachusetts must be censured!" a voice shot out from the back.

"He's taunting the South by presenting a petition from persons who aren't even citizens!" another roared.

"Expel him!" a chorus cried.

Over the raging storm, the Speaker's gavel pounded the desk as he adjourned the House.

With a flicker of a smile, John Quincy Adams descended the broad marble steps of the House of Representatives that day. He did not care if he had become the focal point of their anger. The voice of freedom was about to be heard.

Louisa Adams was surprised to see her husband come back so early that afternoon as he entered the front door of their brick home on 16th Street.

"The House has turned into a hornet's nest, Louisa," he told her. "The Speaker had no choice but to adjourn."

Louisa knew better than to ask who had stirred up the hornet's nest. She just settled him into his favorite rocking chair by the fire, tucked a shawl about him, and walked to the kitchen to brew him a strong cup of tea.

Staring into the crackling flames, the former President recalled the events of the hour before. His smile returned. JQA loved nothing so much as a good parliamentary fight. One famous American author of that time, Ralph Waldo Emerson, described JQA as such a bruiser that it seemed like he "must have sulfuric acid in his tea."

Within minutes, Louisa appeared with a small tray of steaming cinnamon tea (no sulfuric acid) and two sourdough biscuits. She placed the tray next to his chair and silently turned back toward the kitchen to see about supper.

Adams gazed fondly at her. She was his best friend and maybe his only friend, at least in this town. Neither she nor their son had wanted him to return to Washington. Louisa's four years in the White House had been miserable, and their son Charles believed a former President shouldn't lower himself by returning to Washington as a Congressman. Adams himself had not sought this position either, but the people in Plymouth had asked him to run for Congress. JQA saw his landslide election as the hand of God. The Almighty had one more service for him to perform for his country.

Louisa had left the poker within easy reach. He took it and stirred the fire to new life, staring into its flames. Thoughts of tomorrow punctured his mind like thorns on a rosebush.

Yes, tomorrow the House would try to censure him; of this he was certain. He could resign. In fact that would be the only decent thing for a gentleman to do if he wanted to keep his good family name. He could ask forgiveness and retire from the House with dignity. He could walk away and let the gag rule stand. He could take the easy way out of this battle for citizens' rights. As he sipped the tea, these temptations murmured in his ear.

But John Quincy Adams was no quitter. Something inside him told him not to give up. Some voice from deep within his soul encouraged him to keep going. He regarded his office as a sacred trust, and obedience to God was the rule of his life. He believed the Lord had handed him the torch of truth, so he had to carry it even if it meant marching into the flames of scorn and ridicule.

Times had changed, but this 69-year-old man had not. As the last living link with the Founding Fathers of the Republic, John Quincy Adams clearly understood God's plan for the nation. He had been raised on the truths of the Declaration of Independence. As a boy, he had heard the guns of the Battle of Bunker Hill. His mother, Abigail, had read to him from an actual copy of the Declaration after his father, John Adams, and the others had signed it in Philadelphia. He had heard his father, elected President after George Washington, discuss the principles of self-government and democracy more times than he could remember.

The elderly man leaned back and took a sip of hot tea.

To petition for something means to ask, he thought. *It's a request made to a higher authority, someone who has the power to do something about the concern. It stems from the basic biblical right we have as God's children to petition our Heavenly Father. The Pinckney Gag Rule is a direct violation of this basic right.* The words of the Constitution crossed his mind:

> Congress shall make no law . . . abridging the . . . right . . .
> to petition the government for a redress of grievances.

This right to petition belongs to every citizen. To do away with this right in American government would be to knock out one of its foundation stones, thought Adams. He knew this had the potential of weakening the new Republic.

The aroma of freshly made leek soup reached the drawing room. Adams did not detect it, however. He was too deep in thought. His mind had moved beyond the future of the country to the issue of slavery itself.

Publicly, it looked like JQA was fighting to reinstate the freedom of petition. Privately, JQA understood that the right to petition and the issue of slavery were as entwined as a piece of hemp rope. The truth was, this right had been abolished because it involved one issue—slavery. While the immediate campaign in the House focused on a civil liberty, the long-term battle was slavery. The South would one day have to face it. Slavery was a "great and foul stain upon the North American Union."

But for now Adams viewed his lonely work in God's vineyard as being more effective if people believed he was not an abolitionist. As a skilled politician, the Congressman realized that any motion in the House to abolish slavery in the District of Columbia would be sheer folly right now. It would be out-voted four to one. He had to wait on God's perfect timing.

Yet this move to abolish slavery—the abolition movement—was not really new. In the late 1700s, such leaders of the American Revolution as Thomas Jefferson and Patrick Henry had spoken out against slavery. In the early 1800s, a special society had even formed to send freed slaves back to Africa.

The Congressman washed down a mouthful of warm biscuit with a sip of tea.

He recalled the time he had seen a black woman at a slave auction in the District. On realizing she was about to be separated from her family, the frantic mother had broken away from her captors and run up to the attic of a nearby Washington tavern. As Adams watched in horror, she hurled herself out of the window. The poor woman crippled herself so badly she was no longer of use to the slave merchant, who left her behind.

While the Congressman rocked gently in front of the hearth, the words of his mother echoed in his mind. "Of this I am certain," she had said, "[slavery] is not founded upon the generous and Christian principle of doing to others as we would that others should do unto us."

Adams's thoughts turned toward the number of petitions now crossing his desk. He could foresee the day when slavery would create such turmoil it would result in war. At one point he even wrote in his diary, "If slavery be the destined sword in the hand of the destroying angel which is to sever the ties of this Union, . . . a war between the two severed portions of the Union [will result]."

John Quincy Adams was a Puritan at heart and would, in fact, one day be called the Last Puritan. If the nation was deviating from the plan set forth by the Founding Fathers, then God's plan was in peril. Adams took sin seriously. Like his wardrobe, his ideals were old-fashioned—more like his father's and the other founders who had felt obligated to serve their country as part of service to their God.

They had understood that the success of God's American experiment depended on the people's willingness to lay sin aside. Sin separates a people from God. It harms the covenant relationship God Himself has set up. This covenant is based on Christ's Great Commandment:

> "You shall love the Lord your God with all your heart,
> and with all your soul, and with all your mind." This is
> the great and foremost commandment.
>   And a second is like it, "You shall love your neighbor
> as yourself."
>
> Matthew 22:37–39

To the Puritans, sin violated a man's vertical relationship with Jesus as well as his horizontal relationship with other men. For a community to function properly, both parts of the relationship had to be honored. This was the Covenant Way.

At its heart, slavery violated the Covenant Way. The Puritan heritage taught that all men were created equal in the sight of God, regardless of color. Work hard and get ahead and help those less fortunate than yourself. This was the Puritan Way. But among the slaveholders, who held the power in the South, it was different. Their aristocratic traditions were weaving a class-conscious society where some men were treated better than others. Slaves were not treated as human beings created by God at all; they were property. Not only did the slaveholders need slaves to toil in their fields, they also required them to maintain the class structure, perpetuating the myth that all men were not truly equal in God's sight.

Adams realized that slavery was hanging over the country "like a black cloud." It was destroying the lives of those whose skin was black and those whose skin was white. Within his private diary, Adams believed slavery would be the tool God used to reroute the nation back to its God-directed course.

He kept a somber face. "If the House should choose to read this," he held the paper high in the air with his left hand, "its members would find that my crime has been for attempting to introduce a petition from slaves that slavery should *not* be abolished!"

Within seconds, the Southern delegates had leaped to their feet screaming. Their outrage flooded the house like a tidal wave. The gallery erupted as well. Threats and shouts of anger deafened the room. Their own hasty judgments about what was contained in the troublesome petition—which they hadn't even let Adams read aloud two days before—had robbed them of any victory over him. Gradually the tide subsided under the Speaker's loud, pounding gavel.

When the vote for censure was finally taken, however, it tallied 105 to 21, in Adams's favor. John Quincy Adams had won.

Not surprisingly, the Southern press condemned the Northern Congressman for his parliamentary ploy. On the other hand, abolitionists swarmed him with letters of congratulations for his courage, and more than a few promises of prayer on his behalf.

John Quincy Adams had won this victory, but he was under no illusion. The battle was still joined. Just as the poison of slavery had yet to be drained from American hearts, the Pinckney Gag Rule had yet to be pulled out of American soil.

2

FIRE-STARTERS

And you shall say to them, "This is the nation that did not obey the voice of the LORD their God or accept correction." (Jeremiah 7:28)

The pale March sun streamed in through the window of the storefront printshop. An outsider looking in through the dusty window could still see the big wrought-iron wheel of the old hand-powered press. Racks of lead type in tiny pigeonholes had been stacked in front of the editor's desk. A mixed scent of printer's ink, fresh paper, and dusty wood floors filtered out the open front door.

In 1830 the cutting edge in communications was the newspaper. Anyone with a press and something to say could publish one. All someone needed was enough subscribers to cover the cost of paper, ink, and postage.

There were plenty of readers too. From earliest Colonial days Americans had placed great value on education. Not only could the average citizen read, but he or she was well informed about what was going on in the country and interested in learning more. Frequently editors exchanged articles in order to fill up the pages of their newspapers. For this reason, hundreds of papers across the country carried written

25

words from smaller periodicals, words that could be read by almost everyone.

This cozy printshop in Baltimore, Maryland, was the head-quarters of a small monthly paper published and edited by a Quaker named Benjamin Lundy. His paper, the *Genius of Universal Emancipation,* reflected the spirit of the antislavery movement during the 1830s. Lundy felt that slavery was more than an unfortunate social evil. He strongly believed it was a sin against God. But in his humble Quaker way, Lundy was trying to present the issues clearly and fairly.

The editor sat on a stool at the layout table near his desk. The 41-year-old man squared the green eyeshade over his brow. As he packed the leading carefully, his mind sifted through the questions as it had done hundreds of times before.

To emancipate the slaves meant to free them. But how? Emancipation was like a loaf of bread that had risen too high; it was full of holes.

Lundy wiped his smudged fingers with a wrinkled cloth.

Many slaveholders were second- and third-generation slave owners. Even those who disapproved of slavery had inherited it from their fathers, along with their land, and had to live with it.

If these owners freed, or manumitted, their slaves, who was going to compensate them for their loss? The South didn't have the money, and for that matter, neither did the Federal Government.

The editor tossed the dirty cloth on his desk.

Was that true? Suppose the government did decide to compensate the slave owners. If each slave was worth $400 (and that was low—young, strong slaves could bring as much as

$1,000), then the slave population was worth *$900 million.* In 1830 the entire revenue of the Federal Government amounted to less than $25 million. By sheer numbers, emancipation was impossible.

Up North, other factors fueled the debate. The practice of selling slaves captured overseas had been run mostly by Northerners. Although it had been abolished by Congress in 1828, during the thirties many sea captains were still illegally selling such slaves. In addition, the Northern textile industry depended on Southern cotton. Northern manufacturers and merchants were selling Southerners everything from cotton gins and hand tools to cheap clothing and shoes. The plantation owners might be Southern, but it was Northern businessmen who were making the slave system possible—and getting rich in the process. Many Northerners wanted the system to remain as it was.

The Baltimore newspaperman glanced out the window at some passersby. He silently prayed this issue of the *Genius* would touch as many hearts as the others had. His wooden stool creaked as he worked.

There was also the question of what to do with the slaves if they *were* freed. Certainly they could not be cast adrift without help. They had no education, no employment, and no means of support. That was hardly what God would want. They also could not be left to wander the Southern countryside looking for work. In the midst of a slave economy, who would hire them? Desperate to feed their hungry children, would they resort to stealing? And suppose some of the young freed blacks grew bitter and looked for revenge. Would they rise up against the whites? This very thing had ripped apart the

French colony of Saint Dominique (Haiti) less than 40 years before. Lundy knew this was the deepest unspoken fear of every slaveholder.

The editor set the final letter of type and leaned back. His stool squeaked when he stood up.

Even if the freed blacks posed no threat of violence, who was going to protect them from others? Dishonest landlords and merchants would prey on the trusting freed blacks, tricking them into debt and holding them in bondage until every penny was paid.

And what of the slaveholder? What was to become of him and his family? For many plantation owners, the sum of their wealth lay in their slaves and their land. What, then, would God have them do? Plantation living had become a way of life. Was it right to pull their world apart?

By 1830 the antislavery movement had grown to include such men as Benjamin Lundy. They were called abolitionists because they believed slavery should be abolished. These moderates saw slavery for the sin it was and wanted it abolished, but felt it must be done gradually. Lundy presented slaveholders with what he felt was God's perspective. He let the Spirit of God do the rest.

However, Lundy's opinion was not the only one being heard during this time. Other voices were growing louder, too.

The overhead lamp did not throw off much light, so the narrow-shouldered man on the high stool squinted his eyes. It was past midnight, and he had to finish. This was important. It had to be said.

William Lloyd Garrison hunched over the desk. The lantern-lined street outside the Baltimore printshop was quiet. Inside, the only sound was the soft packing of lead type. The 23-year-old journalist hurried to complete the task. At last he had gotten the chance to compose the editorial page, and he knew just what must be done.

Before his arrival from Boston to work with Benjamin Lundy, Garrison had accepted his mentor's moderate approach to the slavery issue. He could do so no longer. Slavery was evil, and it had to be stopped, but not moderately, not gradually sometime in the future—now!

The young man quickly inserted the metal letter *a* in the word *about*. Yes, this was what it was all about. If he could only get people to listen.

Way back in 1787, the question of slaves had created heated debate even during the Constitutional Convention. At that time there had been a move to abolish it, but the delegates from South Carolina and Georgia had threatened to walk out of the convention. Since the majority of delegates believed slavery would die out on its own anyway, they decided on a compromise. They agreed to abolish the foreign slave trade but not for another 20 years. In the states where slavery already existed, neither Congress nor any other body could touch it. The malignant tumor of slavery could grow.

Garrison's fingers flew across the page. In the Northwest Ordinance of 1787, Congress had abolished slavery north of the Ohio River. By 1804 the ideals of the Revolution had dislodged slavery in every Northern state. When Missouri applied for statehood, the storm of controversy thundered through Congress again. Southern members in both the House and Senate had actually expressed the possibility of their states leaving the Union. The thin lips of the young man on the typesetter's stool slowly formed a smile. He almost wished they had.

Garrison was tired of laying the blame at the door of previous generations. He did not want to talk about the problem anymore. He had become convinced Lundy's gradual methods were too slow. Something had to be done. Yes, he thought as he set the last metal letter, the slaves should be freed—right now!

Garrison's fiery editorials were read far and wide. While his tone was the opposite of Lundy's, his pieces were newsworthy. Editors began reprinting his editorials regularly, particularly in the South, where publishers held up his words as typical of the new abolitionist thinking beginning to emerge. Southerners did not like Garrison's radical tactics nor his ideas. This man wanted to do away with their livelihood, at all costs!

When a team of oxen don't pull together, the wagon doesn't go anywhere. In a short while, the moderate Lundy and the radical Garrison realized they had to go their separate ways.

The younger journalist returned to Boston to start his own abolitionist newspaper. The premier issue of the *Liberator* was dated January 1, 1831. On the front page, William Lloyd Garrison sounded his alarm:

I am in earnest. . . . AND I WILL BE HEARD!

In two years, Garrison's monthly journal could claim only about 400 subscribers. Yet his editorials were so blistering that they were widely reprinted in both the North and the South. Southerners disliked him, believing he represented the feelings secretly harbored by everyone who opposed slavery. They coined the term "Garrisonism." The editor was flattered.

In his eyes, his views ought to be adopted by the whole abolitionist movement.

The problem Garrison faced was that, in the 1830s, many people in the *North* still did not agree with him. And anyone who disagreed with Garrison in a speech or editorial would find himself publicly scourged in the *Liberator* as if he had committed a crime and deserved hanging. Eventually the publisher decided that even those clergy members who disagreed with him were corrupt. To him such Churches as the Methodist, Presbyterian, and Congregational were nothing more than "a cage of unclean birds and synagogue of Satan."

Although these guerilla warfare tactics did not win Garrison any favors, even in the antislavery movement, God did use him. Anyone reading the *Liberator* on a street corner or in his home was affected. Garrison's words needled people. Slowly but surely, the issue of slavery was gaining attention across the land.

The wheels of history were turning: John Quincy Adams, Benjamin Lundy, William Lloyd Garrison. Each of these men played a pivotal part in the unfolding of God's plan. Through them, people were beginning to wake up to the slavery issue itself. But more had to happen. People's hearts had to change. For this, God sent a special troop of dedicated men to toil in the abolition field.

3

A NEW
GIDEON'S ARMY

We are destroying speculations and every lofty thing
raised up against the knowledge of God.
(2 Corinthians 10:5)

The early morning mist shrouded the Ohio River so the boat's passengers could barely see. The sound of the steam engine mingled with a wedge of squawking geese flying overhead. As the boat steamed downriver, a flatboat carrying a family of five drifted by, and the father waved. One of the passengers, a tall young man, signaled back and then patted his chest. He felt the small black Bible still tucked inside his vest pocket. Suddenly, the blast of the steam packet's whistle punctuated the morning air. They had reached Cincinnati at last.

Carved out of the Northwest Ordinance in 1787, Ohio became the 17th state in 1807. Steamboats carried passengers up and down the Ohio and Mississippi Rivers, transporting animal skins, farm products, and wood. Countless pioneers were pouring over the mountains and heading west. By the

1830s, the town of Cincinnati had blossomed into a major trading center in the Midwest.

In the fall of 1832, forty seminary students arrived on a wooded hill just above the booming town of Cincinnati. With axes and saws, they chopped down buckeye trees and stacked heavy logs to construct the first buildings. Named in honor of the two shopkeepers who owned the land, Lane Seminary formally started classes one year later. Thanks to the financing of two New York silk merchants, Arthur and Lewis Tappan, this center became the first training ground for ministers in the West.

Nestled among the white oaks, the scattered buildings looked more like a small village than an educational institution. A chilly February breeze stirred up some dead leaves lying near two horses tied to a lonely hitching post. The animals whinnied softly as a young man scurried in front of them across the plank boardwalk. His arms were filled with books and his Bible was still tucked safely inside his vest. While the student's waistcoat did not match his suit and he looked like an unmade bed, there was purpose in his steps.

Theodore Dwight Weld had a job to do over the next few weeks. Even though the clouds cast a shadow over the tiny campus, Weld was not feeling depressed. Deep within his soul, he knew the Lord was involved in this. Little could he have known, however, what an impact the next 18 days would have. A distant steamboat whistle from the river reached his ears, but Weld did not hear it. His mind was on the upcoming debate.

This was not the first time the 26-year-old Weld had been in Ohio. Before arriving at Lane, the young evangelist had preached many times against the evils of alcohol. Like Lyman Beecher, the President of Lane Seminary, Weld believed that the moral destiny of the nation turned on the character of the West. He felt a strong sense of calling to be here. He believed the Lord had placed him and the others in the unique position of being key instruments in shaping the spiritual destiny of the land.

But recently, his life had taken a sharp turn when God abruptly changed his course and sent him to seminary. And now he was hurrying across this small campus to the public debate he had organized.

Weld reached the small, one-story building. Balancing his books, he pulled up the latch on the slatted door. Within the hour, a carefully orchestrated progression of speakers would begin. Weld's opening remarks would set the tone. He wanted to be ready.

Good, no one is here yet, he thought, dropping his heavy load on the long oak table up front. *I still have time.*

Before the first participants arrived, the room was cozy with the smell of wood smoke from the corner woodstove. Fresh chalk lay neatly on the chalkboard tray. A box of cedar pencils and blank paper had been situated on a small entrance table. Rows of cane chairs lined the room.

The tall, broad-shouldered man stood behind the podium. "Good afternoon."

Weld's eyes scanned the crowd. He recognized James Thome, a student from Kentucky. He spotted Henry Stanton and Augustus Wattles among the students from Lane. While President Beecher was not present, his daughter, Harriet, sat in the front row.

He went on. "We are gathered here to look into a question that is beginning to tug at the hearts of Christian brethren across the land—slavery. It's an issue many of us are only beginning to understand. But it's one which, I believe, is becoming the supreme spiritual battlefield of our time.

"The issue we shall address in this debate is: Should the people in the slaveholding states abolish slavery immediately? I have written it here on the board so we can maintain our focus throughout."

Over the next two and a half weeks, Weld presented his case. What was slavery? To Weld, it was sin, pure and simple. To hold someone against his will without payment was wrong. It was a violation of a man's God-given right to choose how to live his life. It was a system dedicated to perpetuating Satan's course for this country.

"Slaves have no power and nowhere to go," Weld proclaimed in a deep commanding tone. "They have no one to help them. They are victims of the system.

"Suppose a slave is told to pick up a shovel but for some reason cannot bend down." The orator held up a wooden paddle with holes in it. "He's beaten with this. His blood and flesh spurt through its holes." The speaker paused for effect. "And make no mistake about it, if this doesn't do the job, a slave owner can use red-hot tongs and brand him—even on the face—to get him to submit."

With patience and passion, Weld laid out the cause to which he had now devoted his life: to bring an end to the most sustained cruelty on the face of the earth. His mission was to persuade these people that slavery was sin and that it needed to be abolished immediately.

The speaker's dark eyes penetrated the hearts of those who were present. His listeners remained almost spellbound.

"Owning another man perpetuates the lust for power in each of our hearts. It would be difficult for any of us to taste such power and not want more of it." The man's eyes looked soft, but his mercy toward the spiritual plight of slave owners did not stop him from recognizing the evil.

"Even if a slave's master is a model of Christian charity, the system imprisons him in the roll of dictator. Where are the safeguards? Who is to say his son will be as kind?"

Weld's powerful words boomed through the hall. "And this is the greatest tragedy of all," he argued. "A personal relationship with Christ doesn't guarantee a person will not fall prey to the system. If someone believes God has ordained the blacks to serve the white people, he can justify any sort of cruel behavior."

Weld stepped around the podium as he spoke. "Dear brothers and sisters in Christ, the system itself is evil. We must help our black brethren and our white brethren. We must do God's bidding and rid our nation of this scourge. We must not wait.

"For us to permit this sin to continue is just as sinful. God is sending us forth to harvest the fields. The time is now!"

In the audience, feelings ran deep. Many of the students had never considered these ideas before. James Thome was from a slaveholding family in Kentucky. He later recalled the moment during the debate when he realized slaveholding was sin. "When once the great proposition that Negroes are *human beings* is drawn out in the Southern sky, the stony heart will melt!" Thome pledged to do abolition's work.

The debates made a deep impression on Harriet Beecher. Years later, she would credit Weld with being the greatest single earthly influence on the birth of her own book, *Uncle Tom's Cabin.* In 1852 this work would alter the course of the abolition movement forever.

As the debate continued, it attracted national attention. Acting as reporters, Henry Stanton and Augustus Wattles wrote daily summaries to such periodicals as the *Emancipator* and the *Evangelist.* A number of Northern newspapers carried their running accounts. These articles fired the imaginations of students on other campuses throughout the North where abolitionist societies began forming.

When the Lane Debate concluded, almost every student on campus was in favor of immediate abolition. The new converts dedicated their lives to the call of evangelizing around the country for immediate emancipation.

In the Old Testament, Gideon was one of God's great commanders. Through Gideon, God sifted out a small band of 300 Israelites who routed out an army as numerous as the sand on the seashore (Judges 7). Now in Cincinnati, the Lord was gathering another Gideon's army, and for its commander He was choosing Theodore Dwight Weld.

During the early 1800s, the Second Great Awakening had produced widespread social reform across New England. Christians began to put their faith to work by establishing new orphanages, hospitals, Bible societies, and schools for the handicapped.

Hundreds of volunteers entered missions work to share the Good News of Jesus with those less fortunate than themselves. The Holy Spirit was at work. People renewed their commitment to God and opened their hearts to their neighbors. Only this time, loving one's neighbor in the Covenant Way included more than building a country. Knitted within the fabric of this ongoing revival was this principle: All men are created equal in the eyes of God.

This debate at Lane Seminary in Cincinnati would soon create a new army of Christian preachers. While these men would speak on many issues of social reform, they concentrated on abolishing one thing: the evil of slavery.

Not only were the majority of the Lane students converted during the debate, they immediately put their faith into action. Augustus Wattles felt called by God to devote his life to elevating the condition of free blacks in Cincinnati. Eventually, he set up the first black school and lending library. Another student, Huntington Lyman, was from a slaveholding family in Louisiana. His tuition at Lane had come from the proceeds of his slaves' labor. He returned home to free his slaves, find work for them, and support them while they gained a common-school education.

Unfortunately, not everyone was happy about what was happening. When Lane Seminary President Beecher traveled back East, his fellow college presidents and friends poured out their fears about the abolitionist societies sprouting up on their own campuses. Beecher was also fearful of the students' newfound zeal for the cause of slavery. He did not want it to divert their energies from spreading the Gospel west. That summer, the Board of Trustees of Lane Seminary abolished the student antislavery society and decided to prohibit all related activities and dismiss any student who was disruptive.

When Theodore Weld returned after summer break, he realized he could no longer remain at Lane under such rules. He withdrew. The trustees did not realize Weld's powerful influence on his fellow students. The majority of his classmates withdrew also. The campus lay vacant.

In the meantime Weld busily forged ahead. Nothing was going to stop him. The believer immediately started traveling across the state of Ohio and speaking out against slavery. Sometimes he stayed in one place for a week, sometimes longer. Traveling alone and staying at the homes of local abolitionists, Weld remained until the Spirit told him where to go next.

Whale-oil lamps hung on either side of the church's front entrance. On this warm summer night, the First Presbyterian Church stood out as the brightest attraction on Main Street. And people were attracted. A few arrived early, then more, walking quickly to be sure to get a good seat. The notorious abolitionist Theodore Dwight Weld was coming to town to speak tonight.

Some were not eager to hear what the evangelist had to say. In fact, the town leaders had met late that afternoon to decide what to do with him when he arrived. The town's banker had reminded everyone that there were already three ex-slave families living on the other side of the tracks. "If Weld has his way," the irritated man jabbed his fist high into the air, "there will soon be more!" The townspeople resolved not to let Weld speak at all.

At the stroke of seven, a tall man with dark, piercing eyes strode up the church's steps and down the center aisle of the sanctuary. It was Theodore Weld. His coat badly needed ironing, and his hair looked like it had not been combed in weeks. But his presence was commanding. Every eye riveted toward him.

Before this preacher could say a word, however, someone roared, "Get out of here! We want nothing to do with you!"

"Be gone, you viper!" another shouted.

Within seconds, the entire sanctuary had exploded. Some people even hurled rotten tomatoes and eggs at him. Weld never flinched, even when an egg broke all over his face. His silence only made the townspeople more furious. Weld waited patiently at the front.

When the bedlam finally calmed down, he announced, "It's too late tonight, but I'll be back tomorrow and the next night and the next until you let me speak!"

God Himself had set this preacher's course. Man could do nothing to stop it. God had called him to persuade these Ohio Yankees that slavery was sin and that slaves must be emancipated. If he had to, the evangelist would return to a place over and over again until his mission had been accomplished. God would take care of him.

In most towns the fury of the mob subsided after the first night. But Weld never knew when it might flare up again. And sometimes they threw harder missiles than eggs.

While he was speaking in Circleville, Ohio, a large stone crashed through the window. "It was so well aimed," he later recalled, "that it struck me on the head and for a moment stunned me." Weld paused for a few moments until the dizziness had passed. He then finished his lecture. For most of the next week, however, Weld did not feel well.

At times a mob of angry whites would wait outside the meeting hall. God never let Weld down, though. Once, after walking through a group of stick-carrying, glaring people, Weld wrote, "The Lord restrained them; not a hair of my head was injured."

The evangelist traveled back and forth across the state of Ohio sowing his seeds against slavery. By 1835 so many local abolitionist societies had formed that a state antislavery society was organized.

Weld was not the only laborer in Ohio's abolition vineyard. The Lane Rebels, as they became known, marched forward to do battle. And it was a battle—a holy crusade. These young Soldiers of the Cross were preparing the way. Weld and his foot soldiers were fighting for a national revival. In just a few years, God would honor their work, too.

In the meantime, the brothers Tappan, who had financed Lane Seminary, had also realized the evils of slavery. Delighted with what the Lane Rebels were doing, they decided to establish another seminary. As it happened, they did not have to look long or far.

The Spirit of God is like a flowing river: When something obstructs His course, He finds another way. In this case, Lyman Beecher and the Lane Seminary trustees had refused to accept that abolition might be God's plan, so the Lord used a clergyman named John Shipherd from Oberlin, Ohio. Shipherd had already set up a small school to train ministers and teachers for the West. Desperately short of funds, the minister approached the Tappans. They were eager to help him. Oberlin College became the first college in the country to admit black students.

The mainline denominations rejected this growing anti-slavery movement because they were more concerned with unity between their Northern and Southern churches than with truth. During the late 1830s, such denominations as the Presbyterians, Methodists, and Baptists staunchly opposed any idea of freeing the slaves right away. Even the Quakers, who were steadfastly against slavery, refused to open their churches to these abolitionist speakers. They preferred the ideas of gradual emancipation and gentle persuasion. Like the others, the Quakers did not want to encourage any ideas that might divide their congregations.

Unfortunately, for the sake of unity, these churches were blind to the growing number of their own members who were starting to believe that slavery was a sin. By putting unity before truth, they eventually brought on themselves the very division they feared. Within a dozen years, the Northern and Southern parts of these denominations had split. From this emerged such groups as the Southern Presbyterians, Southern Methodists, and Southern Baptists.

The end of 1835 marked the end of Weld's work in Ohio. In all that time he had conducted missions in fewer than 40 towns. But in each the taproot of abolitionism had grown deep. Each tree gave seed to others, which grew strong and tall. In another generation, Ohio would become a forest of deep-rooted abolitionist buckeyes. When the whirlwind eventually became a holy crusade to free the slaves, more men signed up to fight from Ohio than from any other state.

✛ ✛ ✛

Once again, the North American continent was witnessing the struggle between the forces of light and darkness. This battle was for the souls of men, and Satan was no more willing to give up his hold than he had been two centuries earlier when the first light of Christ broke on these shores. But God was there, dispatching troops who understood that the most important battle was the battle to change men's hearts.

4

OLD '76

Blessed be the LORD,
for He has made marvelous His lovingkindness to me
in a besieged city. (Psalm 31:21)

On a cool, crisp morning in the fall of 1837, John Quincy Adams was enjoying breakfast in the District of Columbia. As he studied the front page of the newspaper, his eye caught a small ad:

> Slave for Sale. Dorcas Allen and two daughters. Acquired by reason of insanity. Fair price.

Dorcas Allen was a freed slave who had married a waiter in one of the District's hotels. The couple was living a quiet life raising their four children. Then, one terrible day while her husband was at work, two white men burst in and seized her and her children.

It turned out that her late mistress had failed to give her a certificate of manumission, or freedom. Her mistress's husband had known this but had done nothing about it. He had remarried and died. His widow had married again, and her new husband was now taking advantage of the oversight. The man sold Dorcas and her children to local

44

slave traders who threw them into a slave prison until they could be resold.

The hopeless mother could not face the heartbreak of having her children ripped away. Desperate to spare them from the torture of the slavery she had once known, she saw death as her only option. While in prison the woman somehow got a knife. She had already stabbed and killed two of her children when a guard stopped her.

The daily newspaper lay crumpled in the Congressman's lap. He rubbed his freshly shaven chin. What was it about this case that drew him? His heart ached for the wretched condition of this family. Yet if he got involved, he risked alienating his Massachusetts constituency.

The man placed the used white linen napkin beside his empty pewter plate and pursed his thin lips. He wasn't quite sure he was ready to let the public know his private thoughts about slavery.

He picked up the newspaper from his lap and read the front page ad again. Who would help this poor woman? After much prayer, he decided to be the one.

Upon investigation the Congressman quickly learned that the district attorney in the case was none other than the author of the national anthem. Francis Scott Key informed him that everything was perfectly legal.

"Her husband could buy back his family." The lawyer offered Adams a glimmer of hope as the two men sat in Key's law office. "In fact, a local retired general is trying to help him raise the funds."

The general had raised $330. Adams himself pledged $50, an amount equal to a week of his Congressional pay.

He then approached the auctioneer who had purchased the family. Astounded that a former President of the United States was involved, the auctioneer agreed to let the family go at his cost of $475.

Before very long, the Allen family was joyfully and tearfully reunited, thanks to the help of John Quincy Adams.

Without realizing it, the Massachusetts Congressman had weighed anchor and sailed straight into the fight against slavery. He would soon be called upon to take the antislavery movement's helm.

A low moon ghosted behind thin clouds as the black schooner weighed anchor and slipped out of Havana's harbor under cover of darkness. In her hold was a cargo of contraband: 53 Mendi tribesmen, freshly taken from Africa's Sierra Leone on the west coast. Since Cuba's vast sugar plantations needed laborers, planters were willing to pay well for them, and slave runners were willing to take any risk.

On this night, however, the slave runners did not anticipate a certain risk. The black men chained below were not the usual captives whose spirits were easily broken. These 53 happened to be fierce warriors, prepared to die for their freedom. While the captain of the *Amistad* and two Spanish planters were congratulating themselves on their smooth departure, one warrior got free and released his comrades. The tribesmen took over the ship, killing all the whites except the two planters. They forced the two Spaniards to sail east toward Sierra Leone.

Since the Mendi knew nothing about navigation, it was easy for the Spaniards to trick them. As long as the sun was up they steered the *Amistad* east, but as soon as it got dark or foggy, they gradually reversed course. For two months, the ship zigzagged back and forth across the North Atlantic. Eventually the *Amistad* wound up in Long Island Sound off the state of Connecticut. There it was captured.

The case attracted worldwide attention. There were two issues: Since there were no laws governing slave property on the high seas, were the Mendi actually free men who had killed in self-defense? Or, were they slaves and therefore murderers?

While the *Amistad* case attracted worldwide attention, it also attracted the attention of John Quincy Adams. He could not resist becoming involved. After a year of appeals, the case went before the Supreme Court. John Quincy Adams agreed to take the case.

In the cramped basement room in the north wing of the Capitol, JQA laid out the tribesmen's case before eight black-robed justices.

"The definition of justice is the will to secure to everyone his own right," he began.

Taking more than four hours, he laid out the Mendi's case.

"I know of no other law that reaches the case of my clients than this." The orator pointed to a copy of the Declaration of Independence displayed in the courtroom. "This is the law of Nature and Nature's God on which our fathers placed our own national existence. It alone must govern this case."

The Supreme Court agreed. It ruled in favor of the Mendi. The blacks were freed, and the abolitionist press went wild.

By the late 1830s, the voters in New York, Ohio, and Penn-sylvania had sent antislavery representatives to the House. Gradually, the abolitionist movement was spreading through the Northern states despite bitter opposition from Southern-ers and Northerners who favored slavery. In 1837 Elijah Love-joy, a newspaper editor from Alton, Illinois, was murdered. Known for his editorials against slavery, Lovejoy was beaten and killed by a mob of angry proslavery advocates. It was the first time a white man would die for the antislavery cause.

Quietly, Adams wondered whether he might be next. Anonymous death threats were now sprinkled among the petitions on his desk, threats vowing to slit his throat from ear to ear or cut out his guts. But he was not going to let them stop him from doing what was right.

In January 1839, he went public on the subject of slavery. The Congressman proposed an amendment to the Constitu-tion. It would have abolished slavery in the District, given newborns their freedom regardless of color, and forbidden the admission of any new state with a constitution tolerating slavery. The slaveholding bloc protested so loudly that his resolution never even came to a vote. But Adams had made his point. Everyone knew where he stood.

And his stand heartened antislavery forces everywhere. At 71, Adams had become the leader of the antislavery move-ment in America. Halting the spread of slavery in the Union was his goal.

On January 28, 1840, William Cost Johnson of Maryland requested an amendment making the Pinckney Gag Rule permanent. The amendment passed, but only by six votes. The slaveholding states could still muster a majority. But the momentum was shifting. More delegates were beginning to recognize Adams's fight against the gag rule for what it really was—the struggle to regain the constitutional right of petition. Slowly but surely, more Americans were beginning to understand, too. The issue of slavery was at the heart of the gag rule like a snake hidden in a log pile.

In early 1842, two opportunities afforded Adams the chance he had been waiting for. The first came through a petition from Georgia. This one demanded that he be removed as chairman of the Foreign Relations Committee because of his stand on race. Adams saw this as an attempt to irritate him, but he loved turning hoaxes into his advantage. The Congressman introduced the petition and prepared to attack the issue of slavery head-on.

Theodore Dwight Weld, now working with Adams in Washington, mailed a letter to his wife. His aged mentor "lifted up his voice like a trumpet, till slaveholding, slave trading, and slave breeding absolutely quailed and howled under the dissecting knife."

Next, a petition arrived on Desk 203 from 46 citizens of Haverhill, Massachusetts. This one prayed that Congress would adopt measures "peaceably to dissolve the Union of these States."

Uproar!

"I believe a move to censure is in order," Henry Wise of Virginia addressed the Speaker.

When a vote was taken, Adams actually voted in favor of censuring himself! With the eye of a hawk, the Congressman had detected that this was his chance to break the slavery issue wide open in Congress. He demanded the opportunity to defend himself.

The motion carried, the routine business of the House was suspended, and the "trial" of John Quincy Adams began.

Adams rose to make his opening remarks. A hush fell over the hall.

"The foundation of my defense shall be the Declaration of Independence." He handed a copy to the clerk. "It is the law of the land every bit as much as the Constitution. In fact, it *was* the law until the Constitution. I'd like to request that the clerk read it please."

The chamber was as still as the great brass chandelier hanging overhead. The clerk read aloud:

> Whenever any form of government becomes destructive
> of these ends, it is the right of the people to alter or
> abolish it . . .

Adams slammed his hand down on his desk. "Right and duty to abolish it!" he repeated. "If there is any principle sacred on earth, it is the right of the people to alter, to change, to destroy the government if it becomes oppressive to them. There would be no such right existing, if the people had not the power to petition for it."

The old man had moved into the middle of the aisle. "While I may not agree with this petition, these people have the right to petition for a redress of their grievances!"

Not only was the chamber listening, so was the entire nation. Newspapers around the country covered the trial. Special editions devoted to the latest developments could be purchased on newsstands everywhere. Only this time, instead of portraying Adams as a man who had outlived his fame, they were calling him the lone eagle battling to restore a lost freedom and fighting for the rights of free men everywhere. Public opinion was shifting—in favor of Adams.

Amazingly, Adams's ability as an orator still surpassed most men half his age. Theodore Weld wrote, "Though seventy-five years old, his voice is one of the clearest and loudest in the House, and his gestures are the most commanding. Wonderful man!"

Adams went on. "I knew the Founding Fathers personally. I worked with them, and not one of them favored slavery. Presidents Washington, Jefferson, Madison, and Monroe. Each of them believed slavery would die out. Until that time, it would be tolerated in those states that had agreed it was legal."

The orator unbuttoned the middle button of his coat. "In other words, freedom, *not* slavery, was the founding principle of America."

With the trial moving into its second week, an even greater public reaction could be tracked. The mayor of New York, formerly an opponent of Adams, called him "the old hero." The New York *American* hailed him as the torchbearer of independence. He became known as "Old '76."

On February 5th, a Southerner objected. "Mr. Adams is discussing the forbidden subject of slavery," he tolled. When the Speaker ruled against his objection, a second member appealed to the House to rule on his ruling. There was a vote. The Speaker's ruling was sustained, 97 to 25.

"I shall need at least another week more to complete my defense," Adams announced two days later.

Low moans crossed the House chamber.

"However, if the members would prefer to table their motion to censure," Adams's narrow eyes surveyed the crowd, "I will be satisfied."

"I move we call the roll," a member immediately spoke up.

"I second," said another.

The motion carried 106 to 93. Adams had won again!

"Right is vindicated!" trumpeted the New York *American*. "The House of Representatives have done justice to themselves at last, to 'Old Man Eloquent', and to the Constitution!"

Although the gag rule was still in effect, slavery had now openly been debated on the floor, something that had never happened before. Support for the gag rule was growing weaker, but Adams wondered whether he would live to see it actually repealed.

He was getting tired. He promised Louisa he would rest during the recess for the summer of 1843. He relished the idea of watching some sunrises and enjoying the robins in his hometown.

But the Lord had other plans. Adams was now a hero, and people everywhere wanted to meet him. Speaking invitations piled up on his desk. He and his family decided on a long-overdue vacation, a leisurely train trip to Niagara Falls.

Early one morning outside his hotel in Lebanon Springs, Massachusetts, someone knocked on his hotel door. "Sir, my name is Spellman," the horseman said, doffing his hat. "I come from Pittsfield. I heard you were here, and I came to ask if I could shake your hand." They shook hands, and without another word, the man left and rode back to Pittsfield. Adams was astounded. The man had ridden 20 miles just to shake his hand! This was only a hint of things to come.

The family traveled by lake steamer to Buffalo, New York, where multitudes of people shouted as Adams landed. That evening, the town offered him a torchlight procession. When the train stopped to take on wood and water in Batavia, the crowd was so large that the station's platform collapsed (but no one was hurt). They had come to catch a glimpse of Adams and give him a cheer. At Rochester, a huge crowd met the train with shouting, a 21-gun salute, and the pealing of church bells. Military parades and bands, mile-long processions of carriages, and cannon salutes all declared his presence.

None of this had been planned for his trip. When a town heard he was coming, the people did everything they could to welcome him. In Auburn, a torchlight parade of volunteer firemen lined his path. At Utica, a delegation of blacks detached themselves from the cheering crowd. "Thank you, sir," one of their spokesmen told him, "for your efforts in protecting the right of petition and promoting the abolition of slavery."

What Adams had planned as a quiet pleasure trip turned into a triumphal tour, covered by the national press every step of the way. Tears came to his eyes more times than he could count. To his amazement, he had become the most popular man in America! (What a change from a few years before, and how God must have smiled.)

When JQA returned to Washington that fall, he had been strengthened by the words and prayers of the thousands of friends he met over the summer.

The next time he tested the gag rule, he came within three votes of overturning it. Many of his arch foes, like Henry Pinckney, had left the House now. The newcomers in Congress were not as anxious to cross swords with Old '76. Everyone was keenly aware of the enormous public support behind him.

Finally, on December 3, 1844, the gag rule was rescinded. JQA introduced a resolution and it carried, 108 to 80.

Old '76 had waged a battle for eight long years. The right of petition had been restored. And, for the first time in the history of Congress, the Slave Power in the United States was handed a major defeat.

That night in his diary, Adams wrote these eight words. "Blessed, forever blessed, be the name of God."

As Weld had put it, John Quincy Adams had sounded forth the trumpet that would never call retreat. It would be the first blast of many.

5

OLD ROUGH AND READY

I will make . . . a great nation. (Genesis 12:2)

James K. Polk sat down at his mahogany desk in the Oval Office and drew the slender folder toward him. After opening it, he withdrew a carefully penned dispatch to Brigadier General Zachary Taylor. Taylor, commander of the United States Army Detachment, had just moved his troops to the Nueces River in Texas. He was waiting until the President notified him that Texas had been officially annexed into the United States. Taylor's orders were to move at once to the Rio Grande to protect American citizens.

James Polk had been the Speaker of the House. He was now the 11th President of the United States. He paused before reaching for the pen in the silver penholder. As the light-hearted chirping of the robins outside his office reached his ears, his heavy heart heaved a sigh.

Certainly Mexico won't see this as an act of hostility, he thought. *Surely, they're not mad enough to declare war.* Before signing the order, the gray-haired leader swirled his swivel chair around to face the large window behind him. Leaning back, he quickly reviewed the events that had led up to this dispatch.

It was now 1845, and a growing number of Americans believed God intended the Stars and Stripes to fly from sea to shining sea. Polk was one of them. Since Thomas Jefferson had signed the agreement with France in 1803 to purchase the Louisiana Territory, thousands of Americans had flooded the rugged territory west of the Mississippi River. The incredible expedition by Meriwether Lewis and William Clark had opened the door even further. As he looked out the window, the President could almost see the hundreds of canvas-covered wagons now stretching out across the prairie, kicking up the dust along the Oregon Trail toward the west coast. One of Polk's goals while he was President was to acquire these territories.

Many factions in the country wanted Texas to be admitted as the 28th state. The problem was whether this large territory would come in free or slave. Certainly, Oregon and California would one day become states. If they came in free, the fragile balance of power in the Legislature would be upset. Aware of this, the slaveholding states were lobbying heavily for Texas to be admitted as a slave state.

Polk watched a pair of bushy-tailed squirrels scurry around a nearby oak tree. The issue of slavery wasn't the only problem, however. Mexico had refused to give up its claims to Texas and would not agree on a border. The United States recognized the Rio Grande River as the southwestern border of Texas, but Mexico claimed the border was farther north, at the Nueces River. Over the last nine years, this dispute had ignited skirmishes, and American settlers were being injured, tortured, or killed. American hearts hardened as news of this traveled home.

In fact, Polk knew that many Americans were privately sending arms and supplies to their Texas cousins, and some had actually marched south to help. The President ran his long fingers through his thinning gray hair. In 1842 Mexico's foreign ambassador in Washington formally protested to Secretary of State Daniel Webster about this private aid because it violated Mexican honor. Then, President Santa Anna decreed that he would execute any foreigner taken in action on Texas soil.

Just two months later, Mexico's foreign minister declared that his country considered the annexation of Texas a proclamation of war by the United States! As soon as Polk's predecessor, President John Tyler, signed the official document offering Texas statehood, Mexico severed diplomatic ties with the United States.

The President slowly turned his chair back toward the big desk. While a state of war did not yet formally exist, the two countries were about as close to war as they could get. Once this order was sent, he thought, there was no calling it back, and no telling what it might provoke.

Mexico disliked its giant neighbor to the north, so war with the United States would be popular with the Mexican people. But surely, the appearance of land and naval forces on Mexico's border would stop her from declaring war or invading Texas, Polk assured himself. Surely, this action would bring even the proud Mexicans to the bargaining table.

Texans had officially been offered U.S. citizenship, so America had to be prepared to defend her newest citizens. Like it or not, she had inherited this controversy with her volatile neighbor to the south.

Reluctantly, Polk picked up the pen, dipped it, and signed the order. Taylor would proceed south at once to the Rio Grande.

The terrain between the Nueces River and the Rio Grande was hot and barren. As the dry, caking dust blew into the soldiers' eyes, making them scratch like sandpaper, the sun's scorching rays poured down on them like liquid fire. Deadly chaparral pricked their skin and ripped their white sleeves into red shreds.

Taylor's troops did well to march 10 miles a day—for 20 grueling days. The was undoubtedly the harshest corner of America, and one in seven of the soldiers deserted. But for the most part they were professionals and bore the hardship well.

So did their leader. A heavyset, short-legged man, Zachary Taylor had chosen the military as his career back in 1808. His father had served as an officer in the Revolutionary War, and he had grown up in the midst of Indian warfare on the Kentucky frontier. His cool wit and courage under fire had won him acclaim during the War of 1812. In 1837 his defeat of the Seminole Indians in Florida had brought him the rank of brigadier general.

"Old Rough and Ready" was popular among his men, too. He cared for them and they knew it. His common sense and military eye had won him every battle he had commanded so far, and he quickly became a role model for what a true combat general should be.

When Taylor and his men reached the Rio Grande, they set up camp across the river from the Mexican town of Matamoros. The General put his men to work erecting a five-sided fort called "Fort Texas."

With its sparkling white houses and lush colorful gardens, Matamoros looked more like a picture in a fairy tale book than a garrison town with 1500 enemy troops situated on a mud-brown river in the middle of the dry desert. But it wasn't a fairy tale. On April 11, Mexican General Pedro de Ampudia arrived with 3,000 more men to defend the village. He issued the Americans an ultimatum: Decamp and withdraw back to the Nueces River within 24 hours, or there will be war.

In the meantime, the new Mexican President Paredes also dispatched General Mariano Arista to help. On the morning of April 23, Arista ordered 1600 horsemen to the other side of the Rio Grande, up the river from the U.S. encampment. Sensing movement, Old Rough and Ready sent a patrol of 63 mounted dragoons up his side of the river. Although the recon patrol located the enemy about 20 miles north of camp, they were surrounded and defeated.

Shortly before sunset on Saturday, May 9, a rider arrived at the White House with a dispatch from General Taylor. "Hostilities may now be considered as commenced," he wrote. Polk called an emergency Cabinet session and appeared before both houses of Congress for approval on Monday.

American blood had been shed on American soil. America was now officially at war with Mexico.

Taylor and his main body of troops soon left Fort Texas for the Gulf of Mexico. The General had chosen to fortify Fort

Polk at the mouth of the Rio Grande as his home base and then return. Meanwhile, Ampudia and his troops had joined General Arista. Together the 5,000 Mexican soldiers, more than twice as many as the Americans, now barred the road near Palo Alto, the only route back up the Rio Grande.

On receiving word about this enemy encampment, Old Rough and Ready issued an order: "The army will march today at three o'clock. The commanding general has every confidence in his officers and men."

Dressed in dark blue wool uniforms, the 2,000 American troops moved out promptly at three o'clock on May 7. A huge supply wagon lumbered along the rocky road like an elephant. Right behind it, two enormous 18-pounders rumbled in the dust of the 20 oxen pulling them. Slung low on caissons between oversized wheels were other short-barreled cannon. Though they were only 6-pounders, they had a range of nearly a mile. Drawn by teams of six horses, they were pulled behind two-wheeled caissons—containers carrying shot, shell, canister, powder bags, matches, and rams.

As the morning of the 8th dawned, General Arista's troops formed a double line on the spacious grassy plain at Palo Alto. A dozen artillery pieces blocked the center of the road. His prize weapon, 1,500 Mounted Lancers, stood sentinel on his left flank.

The blazing sun glinted off the Mexicans' long line of fixed bayonets. As the Mexican band played *"Vive La Republica,"* the country's banners unfurled. General Arista proudly rode up and down the entire length of his corps, encouraging his men. It was a breathtaking sight.

At high noon the Americans marched into view. "Haw, Buck!" "Whoa, Brandy!" The Americans steered the oxen leading their two 18-pounders into the center until they faced the enemy. Sitting on his favorite horse, Old Rough and Ready skillfully deployed his troops.

Famous for defending the frontier against the Comanche Indians, the Texas Rangers were excellent horsemen and sharpshooters. Today, they waited patiently with their captain, Sam Walker. Some fingered their long handlebar mustaches while others fixed their broad-brim hats or checked the barrel of their Colt revolvers. This was just the sort of fight they loved.

Along with Captain Ephraim Kirby Smith and the Fifth Infantry, Major Sam Ringgold and his "flying artillery" moved to the left flank. (Ringgold had developed light cannon and caissons that could be moved easily and rapidly by horses and well-trained gun crews.) In less than a minute, they were ready to go. The Fourth Infantry under Lieutenant Ulysses S. (Sam) Grant positioned itself on the General's right flank beside Captain James Duncan's artillery battery and the Eighth Infantry.

As the Americans got ready to fight, however, the Mexicans remained in rigid parade formation. They did not fire a single shot!

Let the enemy stand there broiling all day long if they want to. Taylor chewed some tobacco while he thought. *We've got all the time in the world.* Casually, the General flung one leg over the top of his saddle. *If they're gonna give us a break, we'll take it.*

Old Rough and Ready was a wise leader. He realized that half of the battle could be won in the minds of his men. If he appeared at ease, his men would sense that he had every belief they were going to win this one.

The General ordered his troops to take turns filling their canteens at a nearby freshwater pond. Two and a half hours later, all canteens were full and the men were refreshed.

"Advance!" General Taylor ordered at last.

Forward the line went, through the prickly palm grass, shoulder high in places, around the Spanish Bayonet plants with their sharp, pointed stalks, avoiding the chaparral, maintaining an eerie silence. Straight lines, no drums, no trumpets, no sound at all. Steadily, the line kept moving.

On the other side of the large field, the enemy watched. One thousand yards away, 900, 800. When the front rank was about 700 yards distant, Arista ordered his artillery to open fire. But their guns' range was less than 700 yards. The cannonballs fell to earth and bounded through the grass toward the American line. The men simply opened ranks and let them pass through.

At last, the enemy began to advance.

Major Ringgold and Captain Duncan wheeled their eight 6-pounders forward in front of the infantry, but they held fire. Only when they were certain that the Mexicans were within range did they open fire. Shot and shell rained on the enemy like sleet. The huge 18-pounders pulverized the enemy's lines. Unbelievably, the Mexicans closed ranks and stood firm. Still they did not fire!

All at once, General Arista dispatched his Mounted Lancers. As the bugles shrilled their advance, the cavalry whipped around the Americans' right flank toward the supply wagons in the rear. The pounding hooves of 800 horses shook the ground. Dressed in green tunics, blue pantaloons, and brass-plated helmets, the Lancers galloped forward holding flying pennants.

"Into position!" Taylor yelled to Smith and his Fifth Regiment.

"Here they come!" one American shouted at the top of his lungs.

Captain Smith knew what to do. "Form a hollow square!" he ordered his men. "Shoulder to shoulder. Fire on command!"

And then, out of nowhere, Sam Walker and 20 Texas Rangers suddenly appeared on foot like ghosts in the night. "Fire, men!" Walker cried.

Their volley broke into the attackers' charge. Before the Lancers could load their guns, Ringgold's men had swung two of their light guns into position. As fast as jackrabbits, they loaded them with grapeshot and canister.

"Ready, aim, fire!"

The shot cut down the enemy like a butcher knife. The Mexican cavalry charge had been stopped.

The battle had raged for more than an hour when a burning piece of wadding started a fire in the dry grass. Soon smoke engulfed the plain between the two forces. When it finally cleared, the Americans realized that the enemy was closing in. The troops furiously fired their guns, barrels lowered as far as they could go. They reloaded so rapidly they were firing an incredible eight rounds a minute! At last, the enemy fell back.

Sam Ringgold was one of the 50 American casualties that day. The Mexicans lost 500 soldiers. The pride of the Mexican army had been dealt a crippling blow. The Mexicans had believed the *gringos*, outnumbered and poorly disciplined, would break and run. They were wrong.

As the sun set in the west, darkness crept in. Carrying torches, parties of American stretcher bearers searched the charred battlefield listening for the cries and groans of the wounded. Screams of agony and pain split the night sky like a sword.

When dawn arrived, however, the Americans discovered a surprise. The enemy had vanished! Through the dark of night, the Mexicans had quietly retreated back up the road toward Matamoros and Fort Texas.

"Gentlemen, what should we do?"

Old Rough and Ready met with his senior officers inside his heavy canvas tent.

"Sir, I believe we should stay put," a long, lean lieutenant advised. "We're still outnumbered, and in a few days we should get reinforcements from the call-up." Most of the officers agreed.

The quiet, friendly leader rubbed his scratchy chin. His dark eyes considered the soldier's words.

"With all respect, sir," piped up another, "I think we should finish 'em off!"

It did not take long to reach a decision. "Gentlemen, prepare your commands to move forward," the General replied.

Beads of salty sweat dropped into their eyes in the sweltering noonday sun. One, two, three miles. Only seven more to go until they reached Fort Texas.

This time the Mexicans were hiding in an old, dry riverbed of the Rio Grande. Fresh troops from Matamoros had joined them. They now outnumbered the Americans by three to one. Their biggest gun sat squarely in the middle of the road. From the front edge of the riverbed, their cannon pointed toward the approach road.

"Get that flying artillery up to the front!" Taylor ordered from his horse.

In no time, the troops were scrambling to get out of the way of the heavy caissons.

When the enemy charged, the big guns instantly went into action. Grapeshot slashed through the dense, thorny underbrush and the guns poured canister into the enemy's lines. The Mexicans stopped in their tracks.

General Arista had been certain Taylor would not attack a second day in a row. Seeing the disaster, he spurred forward to lead a cavalry charge. The American line held fast, and Arista turned back.

At this point, the Fifth Regiment was locked in hand-to-hand combat along the edge of the riverbed. Before long, Taylor spotted the Mexicans breaking ranks and running back toward Matamoros. Eight enemy cannon and 1,500 muskets lay strewn on the ground. General Arista himself retreated, leaving behind all his papers and personal belongings. In their panic nearly 300 Mexicans drowned trying to cross the wide Rio Grande.

After this victory, Zachary Taylor occupied Matamoros and waited six weeks for supplies to arrive. He was anxious to get going. He had already lost about 400 men, and now amoebic dysentery and yellow fever were claiming more. In fact, during the Mexican War, more than six times as many men would die of disease as of wounds.

On August 4, Taylor and his troops finally got underway. His objective: the largest city in northern Mexico, Monterrey. To get there he would travel up the Rio Grande, then strike south across the uninhabited sun-blasted barrens. At his summer camp on the river, however, nearly 4,000 soldiers got sick. Taylor buried 1,500 of his men. He had discovered that 100-degree heat and high humidity did not mix well with woolen uniforms.

For this march, the General decided not to wait for extra wagons. Instead, he hired 1,900 Mexican mules and mule skinners and named a young lieutenant in the Quartermaster's Corps to oversee them. This lieutenant was Sam (Ulysses S.) Grant.

On September 19, Taylor's force of 6,640 men arrived at Monterrey. It faced 7,300 well-trained Mexican soldiers under the command of General Ampudia.

Old Rough and Ready studied the defenses through his field glass. The enemy occupied the ruins around the city. He'd have to take them first. Immediately he dispatched 2,000 men and a detachment of Texas Rangers under Jack Hays to take the two hills on the west.

On the northeast side, the General could see the enemy cannon covering the streets. Mexican soldiers lined the flat roofs and perched out of loopholes cut into the soft adobe walls. The Americans' first attempt to enter the city failed, and they fell back.

Taylor next sent in the Fourth Infantry. Hearing the distant gunfire, Sam Grant could not bear to be out of the action. Disobeying orders to remain in the rear in charge of supplies, he borrowed a horse and galloped forward, joining the Fourth. Within minutes, they fell back as well. By dusk, Taylor had lost 394 men killed or wounded.

The next day went better. And by day three, the Americans had taken the high ground around the city. General

Ampudia withdrew all his forces to Monterrey's central plaza for a final stand.

Slowly the U.S. infantry worked its way into the city. Grant's unit started running low on ammunition.

"I need a volunteer to get word to Taylor!" the regimental commander yelled.

"I will, sir," the young lieutenant replied.

Grant knew he could go by horse, but he had to cross the streets and miss the gunfire. What he did next would become a favorite stunt in early western movies a century later: Holding onto the cantle of the saddle with one foot and hanging behind his horse, the lieutenant raced across the deadly intersections. Gunshots buzzed around him like flies, but he made it.

General Taylor himself stood in the streets directing the action. The fighting was door-to-door now. Finally, his men broke down doors, and squads of American troopers rushed in.

Late that afternoon, a white flag appeared. Monterrey belonged to the Americans.

6

A WOLF
BY THE EARS

For I will drive out nations before you and enlarge your borders. (Exodus 34:24)

 Could it be that God Himself intended the United States to stretch from sea to shining sea? Americans everywhere were beginning to em-brace this vision. John L. O'Sullivan, a lawyer and editor of the New York *Morning News,* put it this way:

[It is] our manifest destiny to overspread and to possess the whole continent which Providence has given us for the development of the great experiment of liberty and federated self-government entrusted to us.

John Quincy Adams agreed. On February 9, 1846, he addressed the House. "[A]nd God said unto them, Be fruitful, and multiply, and replenish the earth, and subdue it: and have dominion," he read from Genesis 1:28 (KJV). "Americans are called to carry out God's plan as they expand west. We shall make the wilderness blossom as the rose."

Adams was only one of many. This idea of Manifest Destiny included not only Texas, it contained Oregon as well.

On June 15, 1846, Congress signed the Oregon Treaty with Britain. Now, the 49th parallel would draw the chief dividing line between the United States and British territory. But what about New Mexico and California? In time, America would have to address these questions.

God's plan was to establish a people who would live out the principles of the Covenant Way. As Americans journeyed west, the call to follow the example of Christ in dealing with others did not change. However, as the lust for land seeped into the national consciousness, many western pioneers forgot this part of the calling. They saw the western territories as an opportunity to build their own personal ambitions, not carry forth the torch of Christ.

There was more to this migration than covered wagons and the war with Mexico, however. Behind the stage of any play many things are happening that the audience cannot see. The same sort of thing was occurring in America during the middle of the nineteenth century.

As the Holy Spirit worked through such men as Theodore Dwight Weld, Northerners were coming to understand that slavery really was something they should be concerned about. This change in people's hearts did not draw front-page headlines like the war did, but it was taking place, nonetheless.

If America won this war with Mexico, a great deal of territory would soon be added to the nation. What would happen to it? Would it be carved into different states? Would slaves be permitted there? This question soared over the country like a hawk searching for its prey. As the war continued, it circled closer and closer to home.

✛ ✛ ✛

All over America, young men responded to the President's call to arms. Volunteers from such states as Illinois, Tennessee, North Carolina, Kentucky, Ohio, and Missouri poured into recruitment offices across the nation.

In the meantime General Zachary Taylor's popularity shot up across the land like a Roman candle. The people in his political party, the Whigs, began urging him to run for the Presidency during the next election. This did not sit well with President Polk, who belonged to the other political party at that time, the Democrats.

Polk decided to do something. He created a new military position, Lieutenant General, and named Major General Winfield Scott to the post. Scott's rank would be higher than Taylor's. Scott could lead an invasion into Vera Cruz while Taylor remained under orders in Monterrey. No more action for Old Rough and Ready. No more glory either.

President Polk realized that nothing short of ultimate victory was going to end this war. And this meant immediate action. Taking Vera Cruz and ultimately Mexico City ranked high on the list. The last thing Polk wanted was for the war to drag on for years. National elections were just around the corner. He'd never be reelected if people began to get fed up with it.

Winfield Scott was arrogant and stuffy, but when it came to military planning he was brilliant. Three days before the landing at Vera Cruz, Scott took his staff officers aboard the small steamer *Petrita* to survey the beach.

The craft floated within range of the Mexican fortress of San Juan de Ulúa, a two-century-old island off the coast of Vera

Cruz in the Gulf of Mexico. As the craft cruised in the water, a huge plume of water suddenly erupted 100 yards to their right. A second one swirled the Gulf into the air just 100 yards in front of them. Soon, shells seemed to explode everywhere. When the eighth one propelled jagged fragments onto their deck, Scott ordered the *Petrita* to get up steam and pull out of range. He was satisfied. He now knew the firing range of his enemy.

At dawn on March 9, 1846, the largest amphibious landing anyone had ever attempted began. A line of seven gunboats paralleled the beach and raked the dunes with canister and shell to rout out any enemy. No one was there. At 11:00 A.M., 65 surfboats filled with 50 to 80 men apiece slipped through the gunboats and rowed swiftly for the beach. Strains from "The Star-Spangled Banner" reached their ears from the ships behind them. Everyone expected the hidden Mexican batteries to open fire any minute. But nothing happened. By midnight, every American soldier was safely ashore.

The army quickly encircled the city. Had time not been a factor, Scott and his men could have waited until the citizens of Vera Cruz got hungry enough to surrender. But time was a factor. Soon, hoards of mosquitoes would be hatching, and the yellow fever season would be upon them.

On March 22, General Scott issued General Juan Morales an ultimatum: Surrender or else. When the Mexican general refused, the bombardment began.

The task of building special wooden platforms to support the heaviest guns fell to a captain named Robert E. Lee, General Scott's right-hand man. At 40, Lee was older than the other junior officers at Vera Cruz. Clean-shaven, with deep brown eyes, he had a commanding presence and eagerly accepted the assignment. By the next day, everything was ready.

The shells from these large guns opened a breach in the city's walls. "My heart bled for the inhabitants," Captain Lee later observed. "The soldiers I did not so much care for, but it was terrible to think of the women and children."

No place inside the city's walls was safe. Petrified women and children dashed this way and that, screaming at the tops of their lungs. Mortars rained on private dwellings, erupting into volcanoes of fire. Finally, on the 26th, a white flag appeared. Vera Cruz had surrendered.

Three days later a formal ceremony took place on a plain outside the city's south wall. The day was clear and sunny. Two long lines of U.S. soldiers and sailors faced each other at attention in parade dress. The defeated Mexicans marched out of the city to fife and drum. Some turned and sadly waved to those behind. Wives and children accompanied others. As each man reached the end of the file, the sound of his rifle falling on the growing pile of rifles reached those close by. Scott had ordered that there be no cheering or mocking of the enemy. There was to be an atmosphere of complete dignity and respect.

A perfect stillness was maintained. It made a profound impression on a young lieutenant standing at attention in those files. Eighteen years later, at a rural courthouse in Virginia, Ulysses S. Grant would accord the same respect to the troops of Robert E. Lee.

By the summer of 1846, enthusiasm for the Mexican War was ebbing away like the morning tide. No one had expected the war to last very long, and as the death tolls mounted, people increasingly referred to it as "Mr. Polk's War." Polk's health deteriorated, and he was forced to use a cane.

But he did not lose sight of his goals. In August of 1846, he approached Congress for a $2 million appropriation to be used in negotiating a final peace treaty. He intended to use this money as a down payment toward the $15 million (or more) he would pay for the Territories of New Mexico and California. Polk kept this a secret, because he knew something no one else knew.

Back in February 1846, a stranger had arrived at the front door of the White House.

"I will see only *El Presidente* Polk." The dark-skinned man's Spanish accent was strong.

"What is your purpose?" the aide demanded. There was something shadowy about this unannounced visitor and his brown leather satchel.

"Is not for you," he replied angrily in a heavy Spanish accent. "Is private matter. Only for your President."

Somewhat reluctantly, Polk received the visitor and learned he had been sent by Santa Anna, the former *Presidente* of Mexico. Santa Anna had been ousted the year before by Paredes and was now living in exile in Havana, Cuba.

The black-haired emissary opened his briefcase. "I bring message from Santa Anna." While the man's accent was thick, his tone seemed friendlier now.

"Go on," Polk directed as he hobbled on his cane around to his desk chair.

"Our *Presidente* has been waiting for his people to call him home. It is time."

73

The Mexican's English was broken and difficult to understand. Polk listened carefully.

"Our *Presidente* would like passage through your naval blockade in the Gulf of Mexico. If you agree, he will accept the Rio Grande River as the boundary between Texas and Mexico."

President Polk sat up straight in his chair and placed his elbows on the desk. This was beginning to get interesting.

"For 30 million *gringos* dollars, our *Presidente* will settle peace."

Polk's narrow eyes widened. This might be the solution he had been waiting for.

"But—"

The man's words interrupted Polk's thoughts.

"No one must know. Our people will not understand. This must be kept secret. *Presidente* Santa Anna says his regime cannot survive any other agreement."

At last! Polk agreed. Santa Anna could have his safe passage through the Gulf. The arrangement would be kept secret. And the U.S. President would offer him $15 million for the peace treaty. But first, the President had to get Congress to agree to appropriate more money for the war.

The air was as hot and muggy in the House chamber as it was outside on the dusty streets of Washington. Individual hand fans helped. Loosening the cravats around their necks helped too. But they could not leave. The representatives had to deal with the President's request right away.

One young Congressman from Pennsylvania, David Wilmot, did not want to hand out more money for the war effort. In a rare Saturday evening session on August 8, Wilmot felt compelled to rise.

"Tell me, gentlemen," the man began, "just what is the President's motive?" He wiped away a bead of sweat rolling down the side of his chin. "Certainly it isn't to pay for Texas. That's already ours." He went on. "I submit his reason is to acquire more territory for the United States. I voted in favor of this war, but I don't see it as a war to conquer land. Our President does."

With this, the direction of Wilmot's statements abruptly changed their course. "We must not permit in these new areas something that the Mexicans have already outlawed. By this I mean, we must forbid slavery in any new territory we may get."

The portly Congressman undid the button to his tight-fitting waistcoat. "I propose the following provision: If we receive territory from Mexico, we shall not allow slavery there."

For the first time in history, the topic of slavery had *openly been questioned* from the floor. John Quincy Adams had slipped it in through the back door when he attempted to overturn the Pinckney Gag Rule. Now David Wilmot was ramming it right through the front door. From this point on, slavery became the main issue in each national debate. In the 1700s, Thomas Jefferson had called slavery a "firebell in the night" awakening him and filling him with dread. David Wilmot had just tolled that bell.

Like a bolt of lightning down the wire from old Ben Franklin's kite, this proviso electrified the nation. Ten Northern legislatures endorsed the Wilmot Proviso. The legislatures of Virginia, Kentucky, Tennessee, and Missouri denounced it. The South regarded it as an attempt to exclude their way of life from the new territories. South Carolina's John C. Calhoun even asserted that South Carolina would secede rather than submit.

The mood in the country was changing. No longer could the issue of slavery be swept under the rug.

And neither could the war with Mexico. The abolitionists stepped up their attack. They argued that the war was unjust and unnecessary, an act of aggression on the part of the United States, nothing more than an attempt to increase the Slave Power. The political temperature got so hot that the Democratic Party eventually cracked under the strain, splitting into such segments as the antiwar Democrats, anti-expansion Democrats, Old South Democrats, and New South Democrats. In more and more minds, the Mexican War was wrapped in the bloody issue of slavery.

Resistance to the war collided with the President at every turn. In an issue of the *Liberator*, William Lloyd Garrison went so far as to wish the Mexican army success. Horace Greeley of the New York *Tribune* summed it up like this: "We are in the predicament of a man who has a wolf by the ears; it is dangerous to hold on, and it may be fatal to let go."

Word about another victory by Old Rough and Ready as well as Scott's successful landing at Vera Cruz floated home. Polk needed these war victories to keep the Whigs from proving that the war was a disaster and sweeping the Democrats from office next year.

In the meantime there was a paradise to think about . . .

7

SIX THOUSAND MILES

Is the LORD's power limited? (Numbers 11:23)

Paradise. The word appeared back East in glowing reports about the land known as California. And no wonder. Yankees were used to the harsh climate and thin soil of New England. The early pioneers were astounded by the warm California weather and gentle rain. In fact, the early pioneers wondered if they had been transported to the Garden of Eden. The growing season never seemed to quit. All a farmer had to do was poke a seed into the rich black soil, and he could raise such luscious crops as peaches, pears, apples, melons, grapes, sugarcane, dates, figs, and bananas. It was a land of dreams.

By 1846, the treacherous passes through the snowcapped Rockies had only been open a few years. The population density of California was only one person per 26 square miles of land. Most of the 25,000 inhabitants were *Californios*—Mexicans who had moved north to farm or raise cattle or horses. If a settlement was large enough to be a town, it might have a mayor or a handful of soldiers. But for the most part the settlers were on their own. Word of this paradise slowly trickled back across the mountains, but still only about 400 settlers were arriving each year. It took months to arrive by wagon, and it was a journey full of danger. In fact, in 1846, fewer than a thousand inhabitants were from the United States.

However, California was part of Polk's plan. This was part of the nation's Manifest Destiny. And Polk wanted to be President when it all happened. Secretly, he was working out the details, too.

The President ordered John C. Frémont, who was a surveyor, and 62 engineers to draw maps of California and Oregon. After arriving in California, they stayed with John Sutter at his large ranch on the Sacramento River.

According to the rumors, either the Mexicans or the British were soon going to try to take over California. This group of men was not the peaceful surveying party it appeared to be, however. Polk had dispatched a group of seasoned adventurers who sported sharp Bowie knives and loaded rifles. He wanted California.

At daybreak on June 14, Mariano Vallejo suddenly awoke to loud noises outside his adobe house. *What could that be?* the retired Mexican general wondered.

The man quickly grabbed a cloak and rushed to his living room. A scruffy man in greasy buckskins stormed into his living room.

"The revolution has begun!" the man declared. His right hand jabbed a huge knife high into the dusty air.

"What revolution?" Vallejo demanded.

"The American settlers are throwing off the oppressive California Government and establishing a republic!"

General Vallejo was stunned. "Where?"

"Here!" the intruder replied. "Sonoma is our first town, and you and your family are our first prisoners."

The former general was disgusted with the regional government and secretly wanted California to become part of the United States anyway. He did not resist.

Twenty men stayed behind in Sonoma after General Vallejo and the others were escorted back to Sutter's "Fort." Remaining behind, a young man named William Todd designed a flag to commemorate their newly won independence. (Todd's Aunt Mary had recently wed a country lawyer named Abraham Lincoln.) The flag had a star and a stripe, and bore the words "California Republic." With a bear as its symbol, the Bear Republic had been born.

Up and down the California coast the United States Pacific Squadron was now cruising, under the command of Commodore Sloat. On July 2, Sloat entered Monterey's harbor (Monterey, California—not Monterrey, Mexico). Monterey quickly surrendered.

Seven days later, Naval Lieutenant Joseph Warren Revere, grandson of Paul Revere, arrived at Sonoma. He confirmed that a state of war now existed between the United States and Mexico. Cheers from Frémont's men went up as rifle shots were fired into the air. After flying for 25 days, the Bear Flag was lowered, and the Stars and Stripes was raised.

Plans for a two-pronged assault on Los Angeles quickly got under way. Frémont's battalion would attack, combined with naval forces from the west. The threat of this proved too much for the small town. On August 12, it surrendered without a shot. California was now firmly in American hands.

To the south, things were popping like corn kernels as well.

Of all the western states to respond to President Polk's call to arms, none was quicker than Missouri. Many Missourians had kin or friends who had died fighting for Texas's independence. They remembered General Ampudia, who had cut off the head of a rival general and boiled it in oil.

One particular U.S. regiment became famous. It was the First Missouri Mounted Volunteers from Clay County, Missouri.

Under General Stephen Watts Kearney, commander of the newly forming Army of the West, the unit received orders to connect with the Sante Fe Trail, head over a thousand miles west, and take Santa Fe, the capital of New Mexico. Traveling with General Kearney and his First Dragoons from Fort Leavenworth, Colonel Alexander William Doniphan and the Volunteers began their long trek west.

The problem was not in taking Santa Fe, it was in getting there. There was no road. Once the squadron reached the Great American Desert, there wasn't even a track. The men hauled their heavy supply wagons over steep mountain bluffs and scorching sand. They battled deadly coiled rattlesnakes hidden in their bedrolls and swarms of mosquitoes so hungry that many of the men's eyes swelled shut from the bites. Even the animals' hides streamed with blood from open sores as masses of flies feasted on their flanks.

That was not all. The heat from the midsummer sun was like the open door of a blast furnace. Sudden windstorms lifted the loose sand only to drive it like thousands of needles into their eyes and ears. With water holes few and far between, the horses began to die. Gradually the Missouri Mounted Volunteers became the Missouri Walking Volunteers. The men's cavalry boots had not been made for infantry work either. After a while, a vulture could track the army's progress by the bloody footprints in the sand.

This famous march across the desert became known as Doniphan's March, and it did not stop in Santa Fe.

When the capital of New Mexico was taken without a shot, General Kearney left for California to aid in the assault on Los Angeles. Before leaving, he ordered Colonel Doniphan to strike south into Mexican territory via El Paso toward the town of Chihuahua. Kearney assured Doniphan his small company of 500 men would not be alone. General Wool and 2,400 soldiers were marching to meet them.

With new provisions and mounts, the Missouri Mounted Volunteers resumed their long trek south. It was the middle of December now, and it was cold, freezing cold. The men faced a 90-mile journey through raw wasteland at an altitude of 7,000 feet.

On this trip, they could not find a decent place to stop. Doniphan decided they would keep going. And they did, marching or riding into the pitch black of night. Even setting small fires of sagebrush and prairie grass did not help them get warm, for the fires flared up and then quickly died. Before long, both the men and animals began to straggle. Soon their line stretched out for several miles, directed only by periodic fires that shot up into the night sky.

"Halt!" The colonel yelled the command.

The men collapsed on the hard desert stones. With nothing to eat, the soldiers fell into exhausted slumber.

Incredibly, the squadron made the journey without losing a man. On December 25, Christmas Day, they arrived at Brazito, 15 miles north of El Paso.

"Sir! Sir!" The young sentry was out of breath.

Colonel Doniphan put down his cards and turned as the aide rushed into the tent. The afternoon sun cast shadows through the thick cloth onto the hard ground.

"Yes?" he replied calmly.

"Sir, there's a large force of Mexicans. They're coming this way!"

Carefully Doniphan laid the hand he had just been dealt face down on the table.

"Gentlemen, I'm afraid we'll have to stop the game long enough to whip the greasers," he allowed, rising to his full 6' 5" frame. "Just bear in mind that I'm ahead in the score. We'll play it out, after the scrap is over."

After the two opposing lines had been drawn, the colonel rode forward to meet a Mexican officer galloping under a flag. The Texans knew its meaning. This was not the customary white flag, signaling a conference of leaders. This was a black flag with two skulls. It meant no prisoners would be taken.

"General Ponce de León demands you present yourself immediately!" the officer commanded in broken English.

Doniphan's interpreter was a lean man clad in buckskin. A wide-brimmed hat almost covered his eyes. "If your general is so all-fired anxious to see Colonel Doniphan," the interpreter replied, "let him come over here. We won't run away from him."

"We will come and take him then!"

"Come right ahead, young feller," the man smiled. "You'll find us right here, waiting for you."

"Then prepare for a charge!"

No sooner had the officer delivered this message than Mexican trumpets bugled into the air. Instantly, a line of soldiers dressed in green tunics, blue pantaloons, and brass-plated helmets trotted forward. It was the Mounted Lancers. When they reached their places, the Lancers lowered their spears. The trumpets blared again and the riders spurred to a gallop. *"Viva Mexico!"* they cried. The block of cavalry pushed closer and closer.

The Volunteers held their fire. Finally at 150 yards, Colonel Doniphan yelled. "All right, boys, let 'em have it!"

When the torrent of lead tore into the enemy, riders toppled to the ground. Crimson splotches spread across the green tunics of those reeling in their saddles.

Next, the enemy's infantry advanced, covered by the high chaparral. Doniphan's men hit the dirt and held fire. Assuming the Yankees had fallen, the Mexicans rushed forward. Suddenly Doniphan's entire flank rose up and administered a paralyzing volley.

"Now, boys, go in and finish them!" Doniphan roared.

The Missourians charged, bayonets extended, uttering a piercing, high-pitched scream. One day this cry would become known as the Rebel Yell.

The Battle of Brazito was over.

A battery of six guns and 100 men soon arrived as reinforcements under the command of Lieutenant Meriwether Lewis Clark, son of the famous explorer William Clark. The Volunteers resumed their march toward Chihuahua. A few days after leaving El Paso, however, they received terrible news. General Wool and their reinforcements had been ordered north to help General Zachary Taylor who was under attack. There would be no more help for them.

The First Missouri Mounted Volunteers were on their own. To go farther seemed like suicide. They were deep in enemy territory without supplies. Already living on what they could hunt, the men faced another desert. Should they give up?

In the end, the colonel left it up to his men. They chose to go on. They had been through too much to stop now.

This desert, however, would be worse than any before. The sand was so fine that the wind gathered it in drifts like snow. Often the wagons sank up to their hubs. Weak from lack of water, the mules got stuck. The men toiled alongside their struggling animals, tugging them forward. By the second day, water canteens were empty, and the horses had begun to die. By the third day, many of the animals were delirious with thirst. As an act of mercy, the men unyoked the mules and oxen and let the poor animals go.

The column staggered to a halt. The Missourians lay down on the burning sand to die. They no longer cared. This had been too much. Some scrawled notes to loved ones; others prayed. The buzzards overhead circled in closer. Soon there would be a thousand skeletons picked clean, bleaching in the sun.

But then, a strange thing happened. Above the distant mountains to their right, a cloud appeared. And another. And another. It was raining! Before long, water was rushing down the mountainside toward them. Soon gullies and puddles littered the plain where the men were lying. It was enough for every man and beast to drink his fill. One soldier compared it with the fountain God had once caused to leap from a rock to quench the thirst of the Israelite army in the desert. Refreshed, the expedition carried on, finally arriving at Chihuahua on February 28.

Nine hundred soldiers and 150 teamsters faced 3,000 Mexican troops and 1,000 *rancheros* on a plateau eight miles outside of the city. The enemy was prepared. They had constructed a series of massive, connected redoubts between the Sacramento River and a dry water-carved gully called an *arroyo*. So confident were they of victory, they had brought shackles to use when they marched their prisoners back to Mexico City.

Doniphan realized what he must do. The colonel ordered his men to form into a hollow square. He then moved the entire body across the *arroyo* and up onto a plateau beside the Mexicans. This forced the enemy to leave their redoubts and come out to fight.

To the sound of bugles and kettledrums, 1,200 Mexican cavalry swept down from the heights in an earthshaking charge. This time, Doniphan didn't wait. His six field guns went immediately into action. Loaded with grapeshot, they fired at a rapid twelve seconds per round. Before the charge could reach the American line, it was broken. Within an hour, the Mounted Volunteers charged up the hill to take the Mexican fortification.

As the regimental band played "Yankee Doodle," the Volunteers rode victoriously into Chihuahua. They occupied the capital for two months. Every man was ordered to be on his best behavior. When they finally received orders to head home, they left the city in better condition than they had found it.

Warmly congratulating them, Old Rough and Ready arranged for them to depart by ship from the mouth of the Rio Grande to St. Louis. As the General rode past them, the First Missouri Mounted Volunteers sat at attention on Indian mustangs, mules, and donkeys.

Halfway down the line, a giant soldier sat astride a donkey. His legs were so long and the donkey so small that the man practically stood on the ground. Taylor quickly put a handkerchief over his mouth to hide his smile.

"Well, sir, what do you think of this crowd?" the big veteran hollered.

The General burst out laughing. Finally he collected himself. "You look as though you've seen hard times."

"You bet!" the volunteer replied.

By the time they reached home on July 1, 1847, Doniphan's men had covered 6,000 miles and conquered an area larger than the United States.

The wheels were turning smoothly. Oregon. California. New Mexico. Each gear had been set into rhythm by the Great Watchmaker. President Polk, David Wilmot, William Doniphan—each person filled the role God intended him to fill, whether he knew the Lord's plan or not.

The Lord of the Universe was adjusting these roles so that everything would fall in place just as He intended.

8

TO THE HALLS OF MONTEZUMA

Love your enemies, do good to those who hate you.
(Luke 6:27)

Large crowds lined the narrow streets of Mexico City. Colorful pennants and flags were draped out of the windows of the adobe buildings. A dark-skinned, black-haired Mexican peered out of the small window of his horse-drawn coach to hear the gunfire echoing through the alleys. It was good to be back. Oh, it was so good to be back!

Santa Anna emerged from the coach. He arranged his wooden left leg so he could step out easily. He wanted everyone to see it again. They needed to remember. This was his badge of great courage. He had lost it after a cannonball had injured him back in 1838. Yes, the people would remember his victory. This leg would remind them how he had ridden into Mexico City as a wounded but victorious war hero.

He had not changed. He would sacrifice everything for the sake of his country. He had given his leg. He would give his life. Ah yes! His loyal followers would remember his victories

87

at Goliad and the Alamo against the Republic of Texas. Never mind that he had become their dictator. They needed him. He was their savior, and he had returned at last.

Loud chants of *Viva el Presidente-general!* and *Viva Mexico!* swept the area like a brush fire. He raised his arms to quiet the throng.

"Mexicans!" The leader's deep voice carried far. "The Americans cannot decide your destiny!" He straightened his black uniform jacket with its red lapels as he spoke, and he shifted his leg. "Vera Cruz calls for vengeance. Follow me, and we shall wipe out the stain of Mexico's dishonor!"

The multitude broke into jubilation again. They wanted him back. Now they would pulverize the American insects. Now they would win.

Santa Anna mounted his defenses at a place known as *Cerro Gordo,* or "Fat Mountain." Here the National Road from the Gulf of Mexico to Mexico City climbed up from sea level through a series of mountain passes. This was the same route the famous Spanish adventurer, Hernando Cortez, had taken on his march to conquer the Aztec empire and its emperor, Montezuma. Santa Anna placed more than 40 guns on high ground overlooking the road. He extended his right flank to the edge of a steep cliff while his left flank dug into rough, steep terrain choked with chaparral. Not even a rabbit could get through.

In the meantime General Scott was marching toward the Mexican heartland. He dispatched scouts to reconnoiter the territory. One of these was Captain Robert E. Lee. Scott instructed Lee to find a way around the enemy's left flank so they could cut off Santa Anna's retreat.

The tall thin captain picked his way on foot through the dense Mexican underbrush. Though he was careful, the chaparral still tore at him leaving red blood marks on his uniform. Lee finally stopped at a spring to refill his canteen and rest. When he unexpectedly heard voices in the distance, he scurried under a nearby fallen tree. The voices got louder and the soldier scooted deeper into the hollow tree stump. Within a few moments, he could hear the men clearly. They were laughing and talking to one another in a foreign language. It was Spanish. Captain Lee closed his eyes to pray. These were enemy troops.

Suddenly, Lee felt a strong jar. The fallen tree was rocking back and forth. Some of the Mexicans were now sitting right above him! Lee forced himself to breathe in regular rhythm, silently hoping no one could hear the loud pounding of his heart. Squinting his eyes, the captain peered through the wood to spot food and canisters of drink. The soldiers were having a picnic. He realized he was in for a long afternoon.

As he lay motionless under the tree trunk, Lee felt a tickling sensation on his right leg. Within seconds he started to itch. The thoughts in his mind shifted into overdrive. Insects! What could they be? Before long, he discovered the gruesome truth. The hollow tree wasn't deserted at all. It teemed with hungry red ants and vicious spiders. Now they were having a picnic too, only it was on him!

It was nightfall before the last Mexican soldier left. Covered with welts and bites, Lee emerged from his hiding place. To endure the incredible pain, he had forced himself to think up a plan.

The captain rushed back to the American lines. "Sir, if we use axes," he explained, "we can cut our way through. All we need to do is take the artillery apart and carry it with us. It'll be hard, but we can do it!"

The Americans began their work at night. It was accomplished so smoothly that Lieutenant Sam Grant wrote, "Roadways were opened over chasms where the walls were so steep that men could barely climb them. Artillery was let down the steep slopes by hand. In like manner the guns were drawn by hand up the opposite slopes."

General Scott later awarded Lee with a double promotion to Lieutenant Colonel for his expertise, courage, and gallantry during the various Mexican campaigns.

The following morning, a Mexican guard arrived at Santa Anna's large gray tent.

"Sir, it almost sounds like chopping to our left," he said in Spanish. The commander smiled. "We both know that's impossible, don't we," he replied. When a second messenger arrived with the same message, Santa Anna threatened to discipline him for spreading falsehoods.

When the attack came, Santa Anna was not prepared. The American force was so great he withdrew before the battle was half over. He did not even retrieve his personal belongings. The Americans captured his money chest and his formal-attire false leg.

They also captured 3,000 prisoners of war. Scott decided to parole them. This was a wise move. These parolees would remember the Americans' kindness later. It would be easier to surrender to an enemy they knew wasn't going to imprison them.

One evening, an American colonel named Hitchcock decided to write an appeal to the Mexican people. "We have not come as robbers or rapists," he wrote. "In every city we've taken, we have preserved law and order and the rights of your citizens. We are here only to obtain peace." Thousands of copies were circulated, and a number of Mexicans later said they had been swayed by it.

For the next few days, Santa Anna and his companions rode for their lives. At last they reached the capital, 180 miles from the scene of the battle. The *Presidente* had to prepare quickly; Scott wasn't far behind. Before long, the Mexican commander had 30,000 men under arms. In contrast, General Scott had only 10,000. Santa Anna quickly fortified his defenses outside the capital as well as the two points guarding the main causeways into it: a foundry called Molino del Rey and a castle known as Chapultepec.

The white domes of the capital and its towers rose like a shiny mirage from the valley floor. Surrounded by lakes sparkling in the sun, Mexico City was a difficult fortress to penetrate. Any attacking force would have to march down its narrow approaches with no shelter and no way to send out flanking movements. It would also have to overcome the fortresses guarding the city's gates.

Again, Robert E. Lee and his Corps of Engineers were dispatched to scout things out. By this point, Lee's work was so well-regarded that Scott most often heeded his advice. The captain reported that Santa Anna had prepared defenses in three outlying towns and that the most direct route passed by a 300-foot hill where he was waiting with 7,000 men and 30 cannon. Scott swung his army southwest.

In spite of the odds, the Americans once again took the surrounding towns and villages and Molino del Rey. But the cost was dear. By the time they faced the formidable redoubt at Chapultepec Castle, Scott's force had dwindled to 7,000. If he lost many more, he would not have enough to carry Mexico City.

The castle served as a military academy and sat on a hill guarding the gates of Mexico City. By the end of the second day, Scott's troops still had not penetrated it. However, the bombardment spurred many Mexican soldiers to slip back inside the city's walls. By nightfall, the castle's commander had only 1,000 men left, including 50 teenage cadets from the academy.

The following morning, August 13, the battle began again. On the left, an enemy gun kept the Americans from getting close to the wall. Captain Thomas J. Jackson decided to do something about it.

With all his strength, the captain started pulling a huge fieldpiece over a deep ditch. He managed to get it down in the ditch, but the gun was too heavy to haul up alone. Just then a sergeant ran up to help. After they had positioned the gun, Jackson and the sergeant started firing. At that moment, a second captain started pulling a second gun into position. At the sight of this, Jackson's men rallied to help. Within a short time, the Mexican gun had been knocked out, and Jackson's troops were storming the breastwork.

An hour later, the firing suddenly stopped. Storming the high castle walls, the American infantry scaled ladders and at last gained a foothold. The castle had fallen. Watching from inside Mexico City, a despairing officer standing next to Santa Anna muttered, "God is a Yankee."

As soon as the Stars and Stripes had been raised, General Scott dispatched his troops down the causeways to the city. One division rushed onto the causeway leading to the heavily fortified Belén Gate.

Lieutenant Sam Grant arrived first, to discover that the gate was well defended by enemy troops. He led a party around to the south. There he unexpectedly happened on a church.

"If we could get up to that belfry, we would have a great vantage point over the gate," he exclaimed excitedly to another lieutenant. "We could fire on them and take them by surprise."

The two lieutenants gathered their men to take the big gun apart. They toted the gun's parts and its ammunition up to the front door of the church. The young lieutenant knocked on the heavy wooden door. A priest dressed in a long, flowing black robe with a rope belt answered the door.

"You must let us in." Grant used what little Spanish he knew. "Your church will be saved. We don't want to damage it."

At first, the *padre* looked at him with questioning eyes. He then realized what was about to happen. Quietly, the old man swung the creaking door wide open.

Once in the belfry, Grant realized they were only 300 yards from the rear of the Belén Gate. The men worked to put the gun back together. Minutes stretched out like hours, until at last it was ready. The first shot would have to hit the mark. If it didn't, they would be in for it.

Boom! The first shell caught the gate's defenders by surprise. There was instant confusion among the enemy's ranks. Before the Mexicans could figure out where the shell had come from, the Americans fired a second round and then a third. The soldiers ran screaming into the city. The Americans had taken the gate.

In a rage, Santa Anna slapped the general who had been in charge of the Belén Gate. "You're under arrest!" he yelled as he ripped the man's insignia off his military uniform.

At midnight, Santa Anna secretly withdrew under cover of darkness and moved the seat of government north to Guadalupe Hidalgo. He tried to rally the people, but this time they did not want to hear it. There were too many dead compatriots in his wake.

On September 14, 1847, General Winfield Scott paraded in full dress on his horse down the main street of the capital. As he approached the plaza in front of the National Palace, the waiting regimental bands struck up. The cheers of 6,000 battle-scarred veterans drowned out the music. The Mexican War was over at last.

Shortly before the signing of the peace treaty, a final scene unfolded between the Texas Rangers and their arch rival, Santa Anna. The Rangers had not forgotten their fallen comrades at Goliad and the Alamo in 1836. They also had another matter to settle. In January, Santa Anna and his bandits had bombarded the American garrison at Puebla. The Rangers had entered the battle to help. During a charge, their beloved leader, Sam Walker, had been mortally wounded. His long hair, long-handled mustache, and unfailing courage had been their symbol. They looked forward to settling the score.

When the Rangers heard the deposed *Presidente* was hiding southeast of Puebla, they rode all night to catch him. Arriving two hours before dawn, they discovered that someone had tipped him off. Santa Anna had fled so fast he abandoned 17 packed trunks. A flickering single candle sat on the table.

An inkwell had been knocked over across a white satin writing pad. The spilled ink was still wet. They had just missed him.

Santa Anna soon realized that without an escort, he would never get out of Mexico alive. He requested and received safe passage from the American authorities. On December 8, his carriage started down the road toward the coast. A Mexican guard of honor accompanied it. There he would board a ship bound for Jamaica, his place of exile.

The Rangers were in a small village known as Jalapa. When they learned he would be coming their way, they immediately laid plans to kill him.

"It'll bring shame upon Texas," the regimental adjutant pointed out. "You must not do this."

"Just let us talk to him, then," they pleaded.

The adjutant twisted his long-handled mustache and pulled on his tan leather gloves. He knew where "talking" might lead. "No," he replied. "You can line each side of the road as his carriage passes, but you cannot do anything to dishonor Texas."

It was the hardest test of self-discipline the Rangers would ever face. On a gray, chill December afternoon, a rider galloped into Jalapa.

"He's coming!"

Immediately the Texas Rangers formed a long, shoulder-to-shoulder double-file line through which Santa Anna's carriage must pass. In their dusters with their broad-brimmed Stetsons down low over their eyes, they waited for the man who had been responsible for the deaths of so many of their comrades and family members, and also their beloved captain. No one knew if they would hold ranks. No one knew if they would give voice to what lay so heavily on their hearts.

The gilt-trimmed carriage came into view. Santa Anna was in full-dress uniform. Seeing the Texans, his black eyes widened. The color drained from his face. He straightened up. If he was about to die, he would die honorably.

The hard-faced Texas Rangers stared at the carriage with cold eyes. No one moved. No one spoke. The honor of Texas—and the United States—remained intact.

On February 2, 1848, the Treaty of Guadalupe Hidalgo was signed. Mexico received $15 million. In exchange, she agreed to cede California and New Mexico—more than half of her territory—to the United States of America. The border between the countries would run from the Gulf of Mexico up the Rio Grande to New Mexico. It would then follow the 32nd parallel to the Pacific, three miles below San Diego. This treaty settled the question of Manifest Destiny at last. America now stretched from the Atlantic to the Pacific—from sea to shining sea.

In the meantime a discovery was about to be made that would bring men across the continent in great numbers and at great speed.

9

GOLD!

The deceitfulness of riches choke[s] the word, and it becomes unfruitful. (Matthew 13:22)

One bright chilly morning in January 1848, a man named John Marshall noticed something strange. Marshall was constructing a sawmill for John Sutter at his ranch in the Sacramento Valley. Located on the American River, the mill would cut lumber for the settlers now trickling into the region from back East.

The object looked like a piece of shiny metal. The curious foreman reached his big carpenter's hands into the cool shallow water to fish it out. About the size of a pea, the nugget glistened in the morning sunlight. Looking back down in the millrace (a canal that directs the water to the mill), Marshall noticed another piece. And another. And another.

"Boys," he laughed aloud so the nearby workers could hear him. "I believe I've found a gold mine!"

Marshall's laughter soon stopped. After testing the sample, he quickly saddled his horse and sped toward Sutter's ranch some 40 miles away.

"You must tell no one," Sutter ordered, holding the nuggets in the palm of his hand. "I'll send these into San Francisco to be tested. If it's true, I'll have my agent contact the government to secure my claim on this land. Don't want to take any chances."

John Sutter was already prosperous with a gristmill, a tannery, and a general store. He and a handful of men busily prospected the area. Before long, however, a rival storekeeper named Sam Brannon got wind of the secret. Jealous of Sutter's prosperity, Brannon decided to drum up some business. One morning, he rode through the dusty streets of San Francisco with a glass bottle of nuggets in his hand. "Gold! Gold on the American River!" he yelled at the top of his lungs.

The gold rush was on. Almost overnight, tents popped up like wild mushrooms along the American River and other nearby rivers. All day long, men dug for gold, panned for gold, and washed for gold. They could get right to work too. All they needed were a few items: a shovel, a pickax, a crowbar, a dishpan or fry pan for panning, a bedroll, a tent, and enough grub to stay out for three or four weeks. Some owned a mule to carry their find, and others had a horse to carry it. In the beginning, a prospector didn't even need to own the land on which he found the gold. All he had to do was stake a claim, register it, and start working it. After that, it was "finders, keepers." Whatever gold he found was his.

At the news of each fresh strike, more miners arrived from San Francisco to establish their own claims. San Francisco changed almost overnight. Many of the city's establishments closed because the shopkeepers themselves left town to become prospectors. Before long, the seaport was practically a ghost town. Those saloons and dry good stores that were left could now charge whatever they wanted for supplies. The stores doubled and then redoubled the prices of tools and pans.

The merchants weren't the only people joining the throng. Soldiers in the western divisions of the United States Army and Navy jumped ship as well. Even though going AWOL (absent without leave) meant being punished, many took their chances. A month's pay for a private in 1848 was $6. A *day's* work for mining gold could bring $75. No matter that it was wrong to leave the service. Gold fever had struck the armed forces too.

In 1848 it was still mostly California settlers heading toward these golden rivers. That December, however, things changed.

The District of Columbia was overcast and chilly. Navy Lieutenant Edward Beale pulled his dark overcoat around his shoulders. *I'd forgotten how different the weather is here,* he thought, as he strapped his mount to the hitching post. *I miss California.*

Patting his horse on its hindquarters, the man pulled a tea caddy out of the saddlebag. He tucked the carrier under his arm and followed the brick walk up to the massive door of the nearby building. A sign reading "Department of the United States Navy" was posted in the front yard. The sailor opened the door and walked in.

The afternoon edition of the city's papers headlined the news: GOLD IN CALIFORNIA! Beale had brought 230 ounces of pure gold back East. The telegraph wires hummed like a chorus of sopranos. Across the nation, newspapers picked up the story. Almost overnight, the nation woke up. GOLD!

This is how the greatest movement of people in modern history began. All across America, young men and old suddenly walked off their jobs to head west—men with steady jobs, men in debt, single men, men who had families. The '49ers, as they were called, were hitting the trail.

Anybody could prospect for gold, and nearly everyone wanted to try. For once, it did not matter who you were or where you came from. Prospecting did not require a degree in geology. And if you needed money for passage and supplies (which everyone did), all you had to do was sacrifice your life savings or borrow from family and friends.

San Francisco wasn't the only town that changed, either. The island of Nantucket off the coast of Massachusetts provides another example of what happened to American society during the gold rush years. At the dawn of the nineteenth century, Nantucket had been a thriving whaling community. In 1849 however, more than one-tenth of the island's entire population headed west.

Gold fever was as contagious as typhoid fever and as addictive as any drug. Caught in its grip, a man would do terrible things, like risking his own life or the lives of others. Hundreds of men never even reached their destination. Some died in the treacherous seas around Cape Horn. Thousands were lost on the trails and up in the high mountain passes because their wagon trains were moving too slowly to suit them or they ignored the warning of early snows and 30-foot drifts.

No matter. Men still headed west. From 1848 to 1849, California's population shot up from 15,000 to over 100,000. By 1852, it had soared to more than 220,000. In 1849 alone, more than 10 million ounces of gold were mined, and in 1852, the tally exceeded 80 million ounces. From 1848 to 1856, half a billion dollars' worth of gold was taken out of the ground, more than doubling the world's supply.

If the journey west was dangerous, so was the mining itself. Names of such camps as Whiskey Bar, Devil's Retreat, Murderer's Bar, and Gouge Eye reflected the character of the miners. They were rough. Gold tempted them to robbery and fighting. At all hours of the day and night, you could hear men gambling, drinking, and shooting guns. When a miner struck it rich, he might be stabbed or robbed. He could be cheated out of his find in a poker game or by a claim jumper (a person who took over someone's claim illegally). Stockbrokers arrived only to swindle unsuspecting men by selling them worthless stock in gold fields that either had no gold or had been panned out.

Many miners slept outdoors or built winter shelters out of anything from rocks to empty bottles and packing cases. Crushed hands, sprained ankles, and constant backaches plagued nearly everyone. Crowded conditions in the camps and the lack of fresh food added disease as well. Dysentery, smallpox, and scurvy quickly snatched the lives of many.

And the gold got harder and harder to find. A man could work for months and end up poorer than when he started. Soon, miners found themselves digging deeper and deeper on smaller and smaller claims. As they sank into debt, the single prospectors teamed up with partners to dig together or form companies. It didn't take long for these companies to take over. By the end of 1853, the fields were pretty well played out for those mining on their own.

Eventually, Christians migrated west too, and their influence helped stabilize the area. As time went on, more towns and settlements sprang up. Professionals like dentists and doctors realized they could make more money practicing their trade than digging gold. Merchants began selling food and clothing, and lodging as well. The settlers sent for their families back East and established churches and schools among the saloons and gambling halls. They formed vigilance committees (organized groups of law-abiding citizens) and even appointed sheriffs to deal with wrongdoers.

Slowly but surely, the fabric of American society was stretching to the West. God Himself had orchestrated the timing.

Had the gold been discovered three years earlier in 1845, when California still belonged to Mexico, the map of the United States might look very different than it does today. Mexicans would have headed north to mine the gold, and the gold fields would have financed Mexico's determination to get Texas back.

Had it happened three years later, in 1851, California would have become embroiled in the slavery whirlpool. As it was, very few slaves journeyed west, so when California was admitted into the Union in 1850, it came in free.

Perhaps the greatest evidence of God's sovereign hand was the idea that our nation should extend from coast to coast. By the 1850s, this notion of Manifest Destiny had established itself firmly in American thinking. At last the country was geographically complete. She stretched from sea to sea. By now, most Americans were convinced that she should remain this way—one nation, undivided.

By 1853 the days of the '49ers were pretty much over. But for years after, wagon-train guides would occasionally catch glimpses of lone prospectors high up in the Sierras. A big washpan hanging from the pack of an old prospector's mule would reflect the last rays of the sun. The guide could just make out Old Smokey Pete, leaning on his staff as he led his mule, Sarah, along the path. Somehow it didn't really matter whether these diehard prospectors found gold. They were doing what they loved to do—the search itself had become their gold.

10

ALL THINGS ARE POSSIBLE

With men this is impossible but with God all things are possible. (Matthew 19:26)

"Stop, stop!" someone cried. "Look to Mr. Adams!"

John Quincy Adams had just collapsed over the arm of his chair at Desk 203 and was clutching his heart. A few members rushed forward to pick up the 82-year-old statesman and carry him to a nearby sofa. The rest looked on in shocked silence. Among them was one of the newest members, Abe Lincoln of Illinois.

"He must have fresh air," a physician directed.

Quickly, the men transported the sofa outdoors, and even more quickly brought it back in. It was the 21st of February, and the temperature was below freezing outside. They carried the sofa and their ailing colleague to the Speaker's Room.

After a long vigil with his family at his side, John Quincy Adams stopped breathing on February 23, 1848. Calm and serene, his last words were: "This is the last of earth—I am content."

Tolling bells, cannon salutes, solemn ceremonies, and long lines of people mourned his passing. The last great link to the generation that had founded the Republic had been broken. As Edmund Dwight of Springfield, Massachusetts, observed: "The future history of this country is to be molded and shaped more by his spirit than by that of any other man of the age."

Politically, sectional differences between the North and South continued to grow like cactus needles. The same year of Adams's death, the Whigs saw Old Rough and Ready as a candidate of national appeal. They were right. General Zachary Taylor was elected President.

During the campaign, however, the ranks in both the Whig and Democrat parties split over the issue of slavery. In fact, many people were so disgusted with these two parties that they launched an entirely new one, called the Free Soil Party. Many of those who opposed the spread of slavery gathered together under its wings. The political stove was heating up.

Adams's death marked the beginning of an age of great transition in the history of our nation. Not only was the country shifting politically, but technology was having a tremendous effect as well. America was changing radically and permanently.

Clink—clink . . . On either side of the steel rail, a pair of men swung their heavy sledgehammers carefully. *Clink—clink* . . . Their hammers hit the spikes holding the steel rail sitting on top of the cross-ties. The loud pounding clanged through the air. Just ahead, a group of leathery-looking men cleared the way. Some dug out the track bed with picks and shovels while others filled it with ballast, set the cross-ties, and tamped in more ballast to keep the ties from shifting. Next they laid down heavy rails and set out spikes.

"All aboard!"

The moment a new line was finished, it was put into use. If you sat on the side of a hill out West at night during the middle of the nineteenth century, chances are you would have heard a train pounding along steel tracks. With her headlamp lighting the darkness and her throttle nearly wide open, you would have seen the thrilling sight: a trail of white smoke lying flat along a dark silhouette stretching back through the woods.

During these years, the steam engine was rapidly stitching America together. Before this, people and goods had traveled by foot, horse-drawn wagons, and boats. In 1830 the Baltimore & Ohio Railroad made an initial run down 14 miles of track pulled by a steam engine named the *Tom Thumb*. By 1850 nearly 10,000 miles of track had been laid across the length and breadth of the land. The railroad had outrun every other mode of transportation to date.

The locomotive was faster than a stagecoach, could haul more freight than a hundred wagons, and could run all day and night. It whistled between the cities. Railroad lines were named for the population centers they joined: the New York, New Haven & Hartford, the Boston & Maine, the Chesapeake & Ohio.

When the Chicago & North Western Railway made its initial run in 1848, Fort Dearborn (which became the city of Chicago) was just a trading outpost on Lake Michigan. Once, the trip from New York to Chicago took a week by stagecoach; now it only took 36 hours. Within a few years Chicago had become the largest rail center in the country, with 12 railroad lines and 120 trains coming in each day.

This wasn't the only thing on the move. Technology was changing other areas of life just as fast.

The first plows were heavy and wooden. In 1837 John Deere, a Vermont blacksmith, invented a steel plow that radically changed the farmer's backbreaking task. Deere was following an old, unpublished design by an inventive gentleman farmer named Thomas Jefferson. This plow was light enough for a farmer to carry on his shoulders. Walking upright behind a four-horse team, he could now turn two acres in a single day. A Virginia lad named Cyrus McCormick developed a mechanical reaper with moving blades. A farmer swinging a scythe could cut only about an acre a day; now he could harvest six.

Even the farmer's wife got help. A machinist's apprentice from Massachusetts thought up the idea of creating a machine to sew cloth. In 1846 he patented his invention, which was improved by another Yankee inventor, Isaac Singer. The Singer Sewing Machine became the first labor-saving household appliance.

Of all the inventions during this time period, however, nothing compared with the telegraph. Conceived by a Yale graduate who had studied Ben Franklin's work with electricity, the telegraph revolutionized communication across America. Samuel F. B. Morse wondered: If electricity could pass instantly over a wire, what about *information?* While sailing back from England, he devised a dot-dash code: Two impulses, one short and one long, in 26 different combinations to make up the alphabet. The Morse Code is still used today.

The nation was dumbfounded. Almost overnight, linemen began stringing copper wire between tarred pine poles alongside railroad tracks. Train depots soon functioned as telegraph stations. Now, if a boiler exploded on a riverboat in New Orleans, killing eight passengers, New Yorkers could read all about it the following morning. If a ship sank off the coast of Charleston, those in Ohio would learn about it the next day. Americans' thirst for the news only grew.

Thanks to such preachers as Theodore Dwight Weld and the Lane Rebels, the revival from the Second Great Awakening had not died away. God was still the central force in many people's lives. And with God, *all* things are possible! Indeed, during this era of great change, all things seemed possible. Success was in the air. If you believed—and had the determination to work hard—there was nothing you could not do.

God did not forget the helpless either. Samuel Gridley Howe developed the use of Braille and made his Institute for the Blind the most famous in the country. Dorothea Dix made her mark. After seeing a naked, filthy young woman caged in a narrow cell, she dedicated the rest of her life to reforming America's mental institutions. In eight years, she traveled more than 10,000 miles. By 1852, 11 states had built mental hospitals as a result of her crusade.

The Lord was drawing others to this land of opportunity as well. In 1842 a terrible potato famine ravaged Ireland; some 50,000 Irish emigrants escaped to these shores. In 1854 more than half of the 425,000 people immigrating into the United States came from Germany. These immigrants flooded the territories to build railroads and settle the virgin farmland. They brought along a strong work ethic and a drive to succeed.

The cities themselves even illustrated this spirit of optimism. Philadelphia, the city of brotherly love, had broad tree-shaded streets, neat red-brick houses, white-stone doorsteps, and handsome squares. At night, Washington glowed with hundreds of candles adorning the windows of the finest houses. In the west, Pittsburgh lit up the night sky with its iron foundries and rolling mills operating around the clock.

Down South, things looked prosperous too. The willow trees and colored riverboats made New Orleans a stunning combination of elegance and commerce. Horse-drawn carriages, bustling fish markets, and brick townhouses created a perfect place for an evening stroll in Savannah. In Charleston magnolia blossoms and tall palmetto trees gently waved in the soft sea breezes. Tree-lined streets shaded the large houses, giving the city an atmosphere of dignity and charm.

However, everything was not what it seemed. To be sure, a traveler could find big mansions with large white columns and white lace curtains. But there was much more. He could also ride through marshy swamps infested with mosquitoes. He could find small farmers living in cramped one-room cabins and tilling a few acres of land. And he would hear the melancholy sound of three and a half million slaves humming spirituals as they hoed and picked thousands of acres of cotton.

Frederick Law Olmsted, a *New York Times* journalist, toured the South from 1852–1855. He wrote this: "Let a man be absent from almost any part of the North twenty years, and he is struck on his return by what we call the 'improvements' which have been made. Better buildings, churches, schoolhouses, mills, railroads, etc. But where will the returning traveler see the cotton profits of twenty years in Mississippi? Ask the cotton planter for them, and he will point, not to dwellings, or libraries or churches, he will point to his Negroes."

Olmstead could plainly see what the Southerners could not: Slavery was making the South poor. Could everything still be possible with God?

11

A TERRIBLE DILEMMA

*And when He approached [Jerusalem], He saw the city
and wept over it. (Luke 19:41)*

Imagine it is 1845, and you are a Southern Congressman in the United States House of Representatives.

The Speaker lays down his gavel and smiles. "Sorry to interrupt, gentlemen, but it's past supper-time," he says. "Mrs. Thompson doesn't appreciate her lodgers arriving half an hour after they're expected at table."

A few members chuckle.

"I declare this House adjourned until ten o'clock Monday morning."

You are relieved. As a freshman Congressman, you are ready to quit for the day. In fact, at this moment, you'd like to go all the way back to your home and the gentle breezes at March Wind plantation in Beaufort, South Carolina.

As a lad, you had listened to your father tell you about the inner workings of the Congress. You had even dreamed of serving here yourself as he did, but never really thought it would happen.

But this division between the North and the South! It had not been this bitter in your father's day. In fact, your father and his closest friend, a Congressman from Massachusetts, had even been able to lodge in the same boardinghouse. You had chosen Mrs. Perkins's house, just because your father had stayed there, too.

As you walk along the plank sidewalk, you smile. Coming home to a pitcher of iced buttermilk will be the high point of this day, for sure. And maybe you'll get the chance to talk with your new friend, Josiah Tucker, from New Bedford, Massachusetts. He's been in Congress a lot longer than you. Maybe he can help.

Oh, today was a nightmare! No one warned you that you were about to enter a bear pit! With the gag rule repealed, the topic of slavery is now open for discussion. It seems that no one cares to discuss anything else anymore. No matter what the issue, sooner or later the discussion circles around to slavery.

Until this afternoon you had kept silent. Finally even you'd had a bellyful of the abolitionists. You disagreed. Every slaveholder wasn't going to hell. You had to stand up this time. It was a matter of pride. You had to speak.

"Our slaves are like family to us," you spoke with passion. "On Sundays they even worship with us. God has placed them in our care, like a flock. If I suddenly offered them freedom, they'd look at me as if I were crazy. Where would they go? Would I really send them away from their beloved March Wind?"

A few colleagues murmured. You felt certain they understood.

The Speaker then recognized the gentleman from Erie, Pennsylvania. Asa Worthy stood up. "Did your father support the Declaration of Independence?" he asked quietly.

"Of course!" you replied, somewhat irritated.

"Then, he believed that all men are created equal? And entitled to life, liberty, and the pursuit of happiness?"

You instantly saw where he was going with this, and you swallowed the lump of emotion now forming in your throat.

Standing with his hands on the lapels of his front coat, Mr. Worthy continued. "You say your flock, as you call them, are free to pursue happiness. But that's only as long as it doesn't interfere with your own happiness! And your happiness, I'll wager, depends on their doing exactly what you want. Now, sir, would you be willing to trade places with any of these black members of your family?"

You sat at your desk in stony silence.

The Pennsylvania Congressman wasn't finished. "And another thing, my young friend. If you're so confident of God's approval, what do you do with Exodus 21:16?"

You couldn't help but glare at him.

"You see, in *my* Bible, this Scripture reads: *And he that stealeth a man, and selleth him, or if he be found in his hand, he shall surely be put to death*" (KJV). He paused and looked around. "Can the gentleman from Beaufort honestly say that God *approves* of slavery?"

With a chuckle, Mr. Worthy turned to the most senior member of the South Carolina delegation. "Harry," he said, "perhaps you'd better take your young knight to Sunday school, before you set him back up on his charger!"

The House had roared with laughter, with many Southern members joining in. It had been the most humiliating moment of your life!

Now, as you approach Mrs. Perkins's boardinghouse, you don't have much of an appetite. Maybe supper will give you something to do, at least until you can retire to your room and write your wife.

That evening, Josiah Tucker takes a seat across the long table from you.

"That was pretty rough play this afternoon." He helps himself from a plate of yams while he speaks.

"It didn't feel much like play," you grimace as you pull your napkin out of its ring.

Josiah laughs. "You'll get used to it." The man reaches down the table for the platter of ham and helps himself to a slice, then passes it on to you. "Worthy's not such a bad fellow, once you get to know him. He's one of Charles Finney's converts. Joined up with Weld at Lane."

Josiah takes a freshly baked biscuit out of the bread basket and passes it to the boarder on his left. "I gather from your expression you're not familiar with our abolitionist movement."

"Are *you* an abolitionist?" You quickly wash down your warm biscuit with a sip of cold buttermilk, poured from the big white pitcher.

"No," he replies with a chuckle. "Leastways, not yet."

"But could you become one?"

Josiah pours himself some buttermilk. "The way things are going, I may not have much choice."

"What do you mean?"

"Well, your Southern colleagues seem determined to drive all us Yankees into that camp."

Gritting your teeth, you put your fork down sharply. "Seems to me it's *your* colleagues who're doing the driving!"

"All right, young fella, cool down; I'm your friend, remember?"

"Sorry."

He smiles. "The truth is, the problem's not with either side. It's the institution itself." Josiah turns toward the curtained window and gazes at the street outside. A horse-drawn carriage is just passing by. You hear the *clip-clop* of the horses' hooves.

He continues. "Sooner or later, we are *all* going to have to deal with it. We can't just keep hoping it'll go away."

When the man turns back, his smile is gone and his face holds a look of deep sorrow. "Frankly, I don't see how we're going to settle this thing, my friend. Every week, there are fewer and fewer reasonable men who haven't been driven to one extreme or the other. And those who are pushing don't want it settled. They would prefer to see the Union divided."

"After today," you swallow a mouthful of mashed potatoes, "I wonder if that would be such a bad thing."

Josiah puts down the biscuit he is about to butter. "Don't ever say that! Don't even think it!" He sets the knife on his plate. "If you believe in God, then you know He intends all of us, the entire Union, to be part of a noble experiment in self-government. You spoke of family today. Well, *we* are family. A national family. And we'd better learn how to get along!"

At the far end of the table, Mrs. Perkins suddenly clinks her glass with the edge of her spoon. "*Mister* Tucker!" The soft wrinkles of her face move into a frown. "I should not have to remind you that this is *my* house, not yours. When you are in *your* House up on the Hill, you may carry on any way you please. But *here* you will abide by *my* rules. And as you well know, one of them is: No politics at the table!"

Josiah nods. "Sorry, Ma'am."

You try to hide your smile. Your friend looks like a student who has just been rebuked by his teacher.

But you can't stop now. "So," your voice stays low, "where do we find common ground?"

"With your admitting this is a terrible dilemma."

The question on your face prods Josiah on. He eyes the heavy-set landlady who is chatting with the two gentlemen at her end of the table. You both know she is watching the two of you like a hawk.

"You'll have to decide whether your slaves are chattel or family," he says. "You can't have it both ways."

"What do you mean?"

Josiah reaches for the large dish of warm cherry cobbler and offers you some. You accept.

"When the census taker down South counts heads the next time, your slaves will be people—or at least five of them will be counted as equal to three of you. But when one of your slaves runs away and flees North, you want him returned as if he were a runaway horse." Josiah eats a spoonful of cobbler. "Now he has become property, and the laws of property require that he be returned to his rightful owner. If at some time he breaks the law though, he becomes a person again."

Josiah scoops up another mouthful of cobbler and swallows before he speaks. "To get around this, your Southern

115

colleagues claim he's an inferior person of an inferior race that God created to be your servants."

Seeing your scowl, he adds, "But you claim that your slaves can become believers, which makes them not just persons but your equal at the foot of the Cross."

Josiah concludes. "Suppose misfortune hits your plantation, and you're forced to sell everything, including your new brother in Christ. Once again, he becomes property."

By now, the other boarders have left the table. Mrs. Perkins rises and begins to take up the used dishes. She glances in your direction.

Your associate rolls his napkin and inserts it into the silver ring bearing his initials. Rising to his feet, he smiles. "You have a terrible dilemma, my friend. All of your colleagues have. You can't have it both ways. A slave is either property or a person."

He gets up and pushes in his chair. "It's only going to get worse," he adds. "I cannot see how your dilemma—*our* dilemma—is going to be resolved without great tragedy."

12

THE NEXT BEST THING

And there will be signs . . . men fainting from fear and the expectation of the things which are coming upon the world; for the powers of the heavens will be shaken. (Luke 21:25–26)

The story of Elizabeth Keckley illustrates the nightmare of terror that plagued the lives of the slaves in the South.

Lizzie and her mother Agnes belonged to Colonel A. Burwell of Dinwiddie, Virginia. Her father, George Hobbs, was owned by another man and allowed to visit his wife and little girl only at Easter and Christmas. To reward her mother's long and faithful service, Mr. Burwell arranged for the family to be reunited.

Lizzie was overjoyed. Her mother was ecstatic. "The old weary look faded from her face," Lizzie later wrote, "and she worked as if her heart were in every task." The family was finally together.

Those were the happiest days of young Lizzie's life. One morning, her father called her over to him and kissed her. "She's growin' into a large, fine girl," he remarked to Agnes.

"Don't know which I likes best, you or Lizzie. You're both so dear t'me."

At that moment, the master entered the cabin. He held a letter in his hand.

"The man who owns Lizzie's father is movin' to Tennessee." Mr. Burwell addressed Agnes. "He intends to take his slave with him."

The news struck the little family like a thunderclap. Lizzie never forgot their parting scene. The wailing and sobbing. The cries to heaven. Her father holding her mother so tightly they could barely get them apart. The last kiss.

Lizzie's mother was beside herself with grief. The mother's despair grated on Mrs. Burwell's nerves so badly that the mistress demanded she stop.

"There's no necessity for you puttin' on airs," she said. "Your husband isn't the only slave who's been sold from his family, and you're not the only one that's had to part. There are plenty more men about here, an' if you want a husband so badly, stop your cryin' and go find another."

The couple kept in touch by letters, always hoping that somehow they would be reunited in the future. The family had been broken apart and so had their hearts. The fear was reality: A slave could lose a loved one at any time.

Lizzie's story did not end there. One of her uncles lost a pair of plow lines, and Mr. Burwell replaced them.

"Don't let anything happen to this set," the master warned, "or the consequences will be severe."

A few weeks later, someone stole the new plow lines. The next morning, Lizzie's mother went to the spring for a pail of water. Looking up into a nearby willow tree, she discovered her brother's lifeless body. Rather than be tortured the way Colonel Burwell punished his servants, the slave had taken his own life.

The fear of physical punishment and torture was common in the life of a slave. When Elizabeth grew older, Mr. Burwell gave her to his nephew, a poor Presbyterian minister. The minister's wife grew jealous of her and determined to break her spirit. When the minister refused to whip the slave without a reason, the wife got the schoolmaster to do it.

The man took her into his study. "Take down your dress," he directed coldly.

Elizabeth refused. "I won't submit to anyone but my massa."

The schoolmaster grabbed her, tied her up, and whipped her with a rawhide whip until she bled. When she was released, Elizabeth went home.

"Why was I beaten?" she asked her master.

"Go away," he ordered.

"Please, suh, tell me why I was whipped."

Visibly angry, the minister suddenly seized a chair and hit her with it, knocking her to the floor.

The schoolmaster beat Elizabeth two more times. Finally, he could do it no longer. When the wife realized this, she demanded that her husband flog Elizabeth himself.

One morning, the minister walked to the woodpile, cut the handle off an oak broom, and beat her until she bled. The girl was unable to get out of bed for five days.

This illustrates not only the tragedy of the slaves but also of their white owners. Knowing the Bible and preaching about Jesus did not guarantee that a slaveholder would treat his slaves with the love of God. Many Southerners, even Christians, believed God had placed whites in authority and had ordained blacks to serve them. Slaves were no better than cattle. And if you owned one, you could do pretty much as you pleased with him or her. This absolute power hardened the hearts of slave owners like this Presbyterian minister who owned Elizabeth, robbing them of compassion. Absolute power corrupted nearly everyone it touched.

In Lizzie's case, however, there was some victory. Had she belonged to a master whose heart was completely closed to the conviction of the Holy Spirit, her defiance would almost certainly have meant her death. As it was, the minister eventually realized the error of his ways and promised never to strike her again.

In the end, Lizzie was able to buy her freedom with money she had earned on the side as a seamstress. She moved to Washington and secured a position in the White House while Abraham Lincoln was President. With the encouragement of the First Lady, Mary Todd Lincoln, Lizzie published her autobiography in 1868.

Lizzie's story was not unusual. Being a slaveholder was an accepted lifestyle in the South. In fact, owning slaves measured a man's status. A poor white farmer looked forward to the day he could afford a field hand or two. A white housewife in town hoped for the time when her husband could give her one or two black servants. And large plantation owners measured their wealth by the number of slaves they owned.

This was the culture. It's hard to imagine today, but it was accepted. The problem Southerners faced was not what *should* they do about slavery, but rather what *could* they do about it. Cotton fueled their way of life, and slaves grew the cotton. Holding on to their way of life meant holding on to slavery.

Interestingly enough, very few Southerners were actually large plantation owners. In fact, according to the 1850 census, only 254 slaveholders owned more than 200 slaves. However, the economic and political power rested in the hands of this cotton aristocracy. Despite the efforts of the loud abolitionists up North, emancipating slaves meant giving up everything, and the landed gentry could not do it.

But where were the Christians? By the 1830s only a handful of antislavery preachers were even left in the South. Many Southern Quakers quickly realized that no amount of gentle persuasion was going to change the situation, so they moved north. Southern biblical scholars busied themselves demonstrating that God actually condoned slavery. After all, He allowed it in the Old Testament and never condemned it in the New. Southern writers even went so far as to claim that the slaves enjoyed the best of all worlds. "There are few slaves, we believe, in the Southern country," the *Southern Quarterly Review* wrote, "who would change their present condition . . . for all the advantages freedom would bring."

When someone wants to believe something badly enough, all he needs to do is to keep talking about it over and over. Before long, it will achieve a "truth" all its own. This is what happened among the Southern Christians. Since the South could not do away with the institution of slavery, it had to justify it. Many Southern Christians convinced themselves that the Bible permitted slavery. Slaves could be happy. Their lives could be changed by Christ. The ideal of masters treating their slaves with compassion and mercy could be achieved.

How could these Christians not see the truth?

If you place a frog in boiling water, he will try to jump out or he'll die. However, if you set a frog into a pan of cool water and slowly begin to turn up the temperature to boiling, he won't try to get out—he never even realizes the temperature is changing.

This is what happened to the Southern Christians. Slowly but surely, their whole way of looking at slavery was shifting, almost without their realizing it. Southern believers were beginning to accept it as part of God's plan for the South. Gradually, they were starting to think of slavery as a good thing for everyone—masters and slaves alike.

There were a few Southern evangelicals, however, who never came to feel at peace with this view.

Benjamin Mosby Smith grieved, "I am more and more perplexed about my negroes. I cannot just take them up and sell them, though that would be clearly the best I could do for myself. I cannot free them. I cannot keep them with comfort. . . . Oh, that I could know just what is right." A Methodist farmer named Daniel Grant wrote, "When I consider that these people . . . were born as free as myself . . . it fills my mind with horror." The Reverend Basil Manley, Jr. penned a letter to his father hoping God would soon provide "a way to escape from it." And although it was illegal to do so, dying slaveholders continued to release their slaves. As one North Carolina master put it: "I wish to die with a clear conscience, that I may not be ashamed to appear before my Master in a future world."

A few farsighted patriots could see what lay ahead, and it saddened them. Slavery was not part of God's plan for America, and it had to go. The Lord had given the nation time to find a peaceful solution to slavery. She hadn't. Now events seemed to be moving toward a terrible clash.

Yet America had not lost her noble spirit. She still had a few great statesmen, and they were about to enter the scene one more time.

13

THE GRAND OLD GUARD

Remember those who led you . . . [and] imitate their faith. (Hebrews 13:7)

With graying hair and dark deep-set eyes, John C. Calhoun from Charleston, South Carolina, made a profound impression on everyone he met. The tall senator had been Vice President with Presidents John Quincy Adams and Andrew Jackson. His Southern countrymen stood in awe of him, because he seemed able to see farther into the future than most men. And what he saw concerned him greatly.

Immigrants were pouring into America, but they weren't settling in the South. The North and West offered better opportunities. Pioneers were filling the territories as fast as water pumped into a bucket. Soon these areas would apply for statehood. The Southern leader knew they would come in as free states. And when this happened, the Northern delegations in Congress might actually be able to muster the three-quarters majority necessary to support an amendment to abolish slavery altogether.

What could the South do?

The former lawyer from South Carolina concluded that the first thing to do was to stop apologizing for slavery. After all, societies had used slaves since the dawn of civilization. They had been part of American life since Jamestown. Without slaves, the Southern economy would fail. This was their way of life, and it had long been accepted. There was nothing wrong with it.

"Slavery is not evil." The gray-haired senator spoke from the Senate floor one day. "It is our livelihood. It is a good! A great good!"

But how could this be? What about the Declaration of Independence?

Calhoun's chiseled features looked stern. "All men are *not* created equal," he argued. "Even the Bible acknowledges slavery. God clearly intended some men to rule and others to be ruled. No man was truly born free."

Like an arrow hitting the bull's-eye, Calhoun's words struck the South. Planters, editors, and politicians rallied behind him. And in December 1835, the *United States Telegraph*, a Southern publication, issued the marching orders. "We must satisfy (our own people) that slavery is of itself right—that it is not a sin against God. In this way only can we prepare our own people to defend their institutions."

The right to own slaves was now becoming the principle upon which an entire region of the country would soon stake its life.

While the members of Congress still referred to one another as gentlemen, by 1849 they were gracious only to those who agreed with their views. By the end of December, tempers were at the boiling point.

What should they do about California and the lands acquired from Mexico? Bitter debates in Congress all focused on one issue: slavery. Things got so bad that Senator Calhoun urged the South to leave the Union by force.

To be sure, Southerners had talked about leaving the Union before. Thirty years ago, the fathers and grandfathers of these gentlemen of the South had threatened to fight their way out if necessary. But Henry Clay from Kentucky had been able to craft the Missouri Compromise in 1820.

Now, Clay was back in Washington, as one of Kentucky's two senators. He realized how much times had changed. Opposing members of Congress regarded one another as sworn enemies. They would not even greet one another in the Capitol cloakrooms, much less raise a glass to one another at a party or reception.

This saddened Clay. Where were the patriots? Where were the men of reason and compromise? The son of a Baptist minister, Clay could see how close the South was to actual secession. And it deeply troubled him. Despite the hot words flying around Washington like bullets, Clay believed that most Americans wanted the Union to stay together.

He was old now, almost 73. Yet maybe he could do it. Perhaps, one more time, he could point out a road on which both the North and South could travel together. But first, he would have to get the support of one man.

On the night of January 21, the elderly senator left his home in the middle of a snowstorm. Daniel Webster, now the senior senator from Massachusetts, welcomed Clay warmly when he knocked on the door.

The two men met for more than an hour, as Clay outlined his plan.

"In eight days I will go before the Senate and propose a bill that will address all the major issues. I have to cover three things: California's admission into the Union, the sale of slaves in the District, and the problem of the fugitive slave law."

The former Speaker of the House was ill with a serious cough, so he sipped a cup of steaming tea to keep himself warm. The former Secretary of State barely blinked as he listened carefully.

"My idea is to present my proposal but keep my remarks brief, and then give Congress a week to mull it over. I realize—" Clay coughed, "that such a large proposal has never been attempted before."

Although Daniel Webster had just turned 67 three days before, his dark craggy eyebrows and deep smooth complexion hadn't changed a bit.

"What about our friend from Charleston?" he asked in his deep rich voice. "You and I both know he won't let such a bill go unchallenged."

The large candles in the room cast dark shadows on the wall. Still chilled, Clay moved his chair closer to the fireplace. "It'll take Calhoun three or four weeks to prepare a rebuttal. Even if the hearts of our Southern colleagues have softened, they'll probably harden again after listening to him."

The two men could hear the howling wind outside. Pelting snow still hit the windowpane.

Webster broke the silence. "What if I prepare a speech to support your bill?" he asked. "I could have it ready, with printed copies to go to the newspapers. Instead of giving it right away, though, I'll wait three days after Calhoun's rebuttal and then deliver it."

Henry Clay rubbed his long gray sideburns. "I think that would work," he replied at last.

The two men shook hands.

In early February, the visitors' gallery of the Senate was packed. The week before, the senator from Kentucky had presented his resolutions. Today he would defend them.

Slowly, the frail man climbed the Capitol steps. Dressed in a black long-coat with a starched white shirt, Henry Clay paused frequently to cough and catch his breath. The 59 other senators waited quietly as Clay got to his feet. Many of them peered through eyeglasses hanging from long black ribbons. Not a sound above a breath could be heard.

Before he said a word, however, a resounding applause filled the hall. The crowd knew they were about to hear one of the greatest speakers of all time. One day, they would tell the story of the Omnibus Bill to their grandchildren.

The orator began his speech. He wasn't as bright eyed as he had been the week before, but he glanced around the room. Despite his continuing illness, a feeling of healthy satisfaction swept over him.

"As you remember, last week I offered a series of resolutions as a friendly arrangement between slave states and free," Clay began.

The tall thin man proceeded to list the resolutions once again. First, Congress would admit California as a free state. The remaining territories acquired from Mexico would be set up without any provisions for slavery. Clay paused a moment, hoping this idea would sink in and satisfy his Northern colleagues.

Secondly, slaves could be brought into the District of Columbia but not to be sold. There would be no more slave-block auctions or chained slaves marching past the Capitol.

As he spoke, he watched the reaction of his Southern associates. *They should be able to swallow this one,* he thought.

And finally, Congress would pass a new fugitive slave law. This would enable slave owners to hunt for their runaway slaves up North. The speaker knew this would get the approval of his Southern colleagues.

The senator arranged his black bow tie with its trailing ends as he went over each point. At last he concluded. "I solemnly pause, gentlemen, at the edge of the precipice, before the fearful and disastrous leap is taken into the yawning abyss below."

The man raised his eyes toward heaven. "If dissolution of our great Union should occur, I pray I shall not survive to behold it."

Four weeks later, John C. Calhoun responded. On Monday, March 4, the 67-year-old senator entered the chamber slowly on the arms of Senator James Mason of Virginia and his old friend John Hamilton. Wheezing and thin, the once tall, vibrant senator was now stooped over. His cheeks were hollow and his eyes sunken. Some of the onlookers gasped. The senator was very sick. He was too weak to deliver the speech himself; Mason read it for him.

Calhoun's words were as cold and hard as diamonds. "Slavery is a positive good," he argued. "Southerners have the right to own slaves and to take them into the new territories and states. The Union itself is being endangered by these constant attacks on an institution that has been around since the founding of the country," he maintained.

To everyone's surprise, the Southern senator offered his own proposal. "I propose we adopt an amendment to the Constitution. This would require that *two* Presidents be elected from now on, and would grant each state the right to veto any national legislation with which it disagreed."

Calhoun thought his words would kindle the smoldering fire in the hearts of his Southern comrades. But they did not. He had gone too far. The South wasn't ready to secede. Not one Southern senator seconded his motion.

Three days later, as planned, Daniel Webster responded. He had copies of his speech ready for distribution as soon as he delivered it on the Senate floor. Webster had been ill for some time too, yet his mind could not rest. The future of the nation was at stake.

All of Washington, from ladies in fine silks to reporters with note pads, occupied the gallery and leaned over the banisters to hear. Although the March weather was crisp, the Senate stove needed no fire. The room was packed.

As he rose to his feet, the old statesman mopped his brow. If this was going to be his last speech, he was determined that it would be his best. Although his dark hair was mostly gone, his large dark eyes were filled with the passion he felt.

"Mr. President, I wish to speak today, not as a Massachusetts man, not as a Northern man, but as an American. I speak today for the preservation of the Union."

At the sound of a rustle, all eyes turned toward the entrance to the Senate chamber. A tall gaunt form in a long black cloak and flowing white hair appeared. John C. Calhoun sank into his seat. It had taken all of his strength to get there.

For more than three hours, Webster went on. He never once looked at his notes. And his words reached the hearts of his listeners.

"Never did there devolve, on any generation of men, higher trusts than now devolve upon us for the preservation of this

Constitution, and the harmony and peace of all who are destined to live under it. Let us make our generation one of the strongest, and the brightest link in that golden chain which is destined, I fully believe, to grapple the people of all the States to this Constitution for ages to come!"

With this, he sat down. An ovation rolled across the chamber and seemed to go on forever. Daniel Webster's speech had steered the people back to their moorings, reminding them that they were Americans first. The Union was a sacred trust, a covenant, and against all odds it *must* endure.

By the end of March, more than 120,000 copies of Webster's speech had been circulated. In its wake, the rising tide of secession subsided.

On March 31, 1849, John C. Calhoun died. The South mourned him. For now at least, the strong voice of secession had been silenced.

The Compromise of 1850 became law. Bonfires, parades, speeches, and crowds shouted, "The Union is saved!" They did not exaggerate. Once again, the contest over slavery had been put to sleep—but only for awhile.

Everyone wanted to believe the Compromise had resolved their differences, but it had not. In truth, the South adopted a policy of "let's wait and see."

What they were waiting for involved the new Fugitive Slave Act. Would the North honor it? It did not take long for the South to find out.

14

FREEDOM ROAD

It was for freedom that Christ set us free.
(Galatians 5:1)

For slaves sweating in the cotton fields, the pull of freedom was strong. They ran away for many reasons: harsh treatment, brutal whippings, fear of losing their families, being sold. Escaping was not the hard part—there were no stone walls or barbed wire holding them on the plantations. Yet many blacks stayed, because not getting recaptured *was* hard. They owned nothing and had little or no money. There were no paved roads to freedom. How could the runaways avoid the slave catchers and tracking dogs and make it hundreds of miles north? Here are some of their stories.

One slave woman told of trudging through the snake-infested swamps in Mississippi. Whenever she heard the barking hounds closing in, she would lunge into the murky water and wade through it to throw the animals off the scent. One time, the dogs were catching up to her, but there wasn't any water.

132

"God, please protect me," she pleaded as she knelt in the gooey mud.

Calmly, she waited for the hounds. Within minutes, they found her. As soon as the ferocious animals bounded up, the runaway reached into her cotton dress pocket. Fetching out her last piece of cornbread, she held it out to them. Oddly, the bloodhounds did not attack. Instead they began playfully jumping around her. The dogs ate the morsels and scampered into the woods. The slave woman finally made it all the way to Canada.

During the 1840s and 50s, a growing group of men and women—whites and free blacks—hid runaways in their homes, feeding them, clothing them, and passing them along to other safe houses. Many of them believed they had been called by God to do this. Risking their reputations, their freedom, and even their lives, they faced stiff fines and possibly prison if they got caught. Their homes were "depots" on what became known as the "Underground Railroad," or UGRR.

In 1831, a Kentucky slave named Tice Davids escaped by swimming the Ohio River. When his master came after him, Tice had vanished without a trace. Mystified, his master said he must have gone off on an "underground road." With the retelling of the story, the phrase became popular, eventually expanding to Underground Railroad.

In 1849 a slave named Harriet Tubman escaped from a Maryland plantation after learning she was about to be sold farther South, where slaves were literally worked to death.

A white woman befriended her, and she passed on up the UGRR until she reached Pennsylvania where she was free. In Philadelphia, this former slave started saving her money. In 1850 she slipped back down into Maryland to rescue her sister and her sister's two children. A few months later she returned to get her brother and two others.

Altogether, this one black woman made 19 trips South and rescued more than 300 slaves. With the code name Moses, she led many of her people out of bondage. A Christian of deep faith, she fearlessly went wherever she felt God was leading her.

On a mission, she required strict obedience from her charges. If a fugitive began to get cold feet and wanted to get off Freedom Road and go back and give up, she could not risk him betraying the rest of their party to the authorities. So she would shore up his courage with her Colt. Pointing her long-barreled revolver at him, she would say, "Dead niggers tell no tales; you go, or you die." She never had to kill any of them, but they never doubted that she would.

In November 1856, the former slave was leading four runaways along a dirt road. All of a sudden she stopped.

"Shh . . ."

Motioning to them with her long fingers, Moses quickly directed them off the road and into the woods. Down a steep embankment, the group discovered an icy river. Shivering and cold, the leader waded across the treacherous current first. Her frightened people followed. The next morning, the group returned to the road. Sure enough, they found the ashes of a campfire. A slave-catching patrol had been on the prowl right in that spot.

Another famous person on the UGRR was a Quaker school-teacher named Levi Coffin. Born and raised in North Carolina, Levi witnessed a terrifying sight when he was only seven. A line of slaves shackled to one another by their necks shuffled down a dirt road ahead of a white trader on horseback. The sight affected him greatly. With his father's blessing, the boy began to sneak food to runaways hiding in the woods near their farm.

In 1828 Levi dedicated his life to helping the slaves. He did it because of what he saw while watching a slave auction in nearby Lambertville, North Carolina.

"We has another good one here!" The voice of a man with a scar on his cheek crackled over the noise of the crowd.

A young black girl, who was holding her 1-year-old child in her arms, walked up the steps to a wooden auction platform. The auctioneer nudged the woman forward with the end of a pointed stick.

"Good cook, house servant, field hand." The man poked her to make her turn around. "See how fine she's built!" he announced, thrusting the stick at her thin cotton dress. "Dare say she's a fine Christian, too. Yep. What am I bid for this here valuable piece of property?"

Levi listened as various men in the crowd bid for her. A tall man wearing a brown leather jacket and tan hat purchased her. The slave stepped off the platform with her baby.

"Please, suh, m'baby." Levi heard the woman address her new master. The man stood there stiffly, ignoring her.

"And now, we has the boy child!" The auctioneer's brassy voice caught Levi's attention. "What's the bid for him? Long service. Good return on your investment." (A slaveholder could buy a child for very little, give it to one of his slaves to raise, and have a valuable field hand in twelve or thirteen years.)

"Please, massa, buy my child!" The panic-stricken mother had fallen to her knees.

"Please!" she begged as she pulled at the hem of his pants.

The man never even raised his arm to bid. Another man bought the little child, and when he came over to take his property, the girl was frantic.

"No, suh, m' baby. Please don' take m'baby!"

Her new master grabbed her and tore the child away from her.

"My child! My child!" She screamed at the top of her lungs, as two men dragged her away through the watching crowd.

For weeks, the woman's piercing cries haunted Levi. He committed the rest of his life to the UGRR and eventually became known as its "president."

One black girl he helped was Eliza Harris, a slave from Kentucky. Eliza had learned that her master planned to sell her little boy. On a cold wintry night, the young mother slipped away with her son and rushed toward the Ohio River. The Ohio formed the natural border between Kentucky and the free state of Ohio. Normally frozen solid, this night the river was littered with huge pieces of ice.

In the chill of the night air, the frightened mother could hear the bloodhounds barking behind her. Clutching her son, the desperate girl leaped from one large cake of floating ice to another. Shivering and soaked to the waist, she made it to the Ohio side. A stranger who had been watching helped her to a nearby house where she found safety. Eliza and her little boy eventually wound up at Levi's.

In 1852 the story of Eliza Harris's daring escape burst upon the world in the book entitled *Uncle Tom's Cabin* by Harriet Beecher Stowe. More than any other single thing, this phenomenal bestseller woke up the nation to the horrors of slavery.

The daughter of Lane Seminary President Lyman Beecher, Harriet had attended the abolition debates with Theodore Dwight Weld. She lived in Cincinnati with her husband, Reverend Calvin Stowe, a member of the seminary's faculty. Harriet had experienced the terrors of slavery first-hand: Her free black maid had been kidnapped by men who tried to sell her back into slavery. Harriet had also witnessed the horrors of a white mob's attempt to steal black children from the free black community in Cincinnati.

In 1850 an incident occurred that propelled her into doing something about her convictions against slavery. Her husband had accepted a teaching position in Maine. On the way there, the couple visited Hattie's brother and sister-in-law in Boston. The new Fugitive Slave Act had just been passed by Congress. Bostonians were erupting with anger. Free blacks were being kidnapped and sold south.

Hattie's sister-in-law later wrote her. "Hattie," she said, "if I could use a pen as you can, I would write something which would make this whole nation feel what an accursed thing slavery is." Mrs. Stowe crushed the letter in her hand. "I will write something! I will, if I live!"

God's inspiration was with her all the way. People wept as they read about a cruel overseer named Simon Legree beating to death a kindly old slave named Uncle Tom. Their hearts reached out when the young Negro girl, Eliza, clutching her son, escaped across the frozen Ohio River in the night. When readers finished *Uncle Tom's Cabin,* they could never look at slavery the same way again.

In March 1852, the book's first printing of 5,000 copies sold out in two days. The next printing sold out as quickly. Soon three presses were running 24 hours a day and they still could not keep up with the demand. By year's end, 300,000 copies had been sold. Today, that would make a book a major bestseller. A century and a half ago, such a thing was unheard of. Eventually her book was translated into 25 foreign languages, including Russian and Japanese.

It was said that with this one book Harriet Beecher Stowe created 2 million abolitionists. President Abraham Lincoln would one day greet her as "the little lady who started the great war." He wasn't far from the truth.

The new strict Fugitive Slave Act only made matters worse. Under this law, a slaveholder could hire an agent to go north to recapture runaway slaves. For fairness, Federal commissioners were appointed to decide each case or dispute brought before them. But they had a clear incentive to decide in favor of the whites involved in the cases. They were paid ten dollars for each runaway returned to slavery and only five dollars for ordering a runaway's release. Furthermore, any marshall refusing to arrest a fugitive slave was liable to a whopping thousand-dollar fine. And, if you got caught helping a fugitive, you'd be charged *two* thousand (1850) dollars *plus* six months in jail!

Reaction up North was swift and strong. Not since the War for Independence had groups of Americans promoted civil disobedience. They did now. Meeting secretly and forming vigilance committees, they conspired to do everything in their power to stop the slave hunters. In Boston, tempers flared so high against the fugitive slave law that men such as Charles Francis Adams (the son of John Quincy Adams) and Charles Sumner, a U.S. senator, joined forces with people like Samuel Gridley Howe, founder of the Perkins School for the Blind, to resist the law. No longer could men of good standing in the community remain neutral.

In New England, many heeded the words of Gilbert Haven, a Yankee preacher. "If you wish for the cause of God to prevail, you must enroll yourself among the Fugitive Slave Law's opponents . . ." The New York *Evangelist,* a Christian journal, heralded that no human law could bind the conscience of the people to such revolting work as helping recapture slaves.

Before the new law had been on the books a month, runaway slaves had been arrested in Detroit, Harrisburg, and Philadelphia. Cities throughout the North held meetings about what to do. They had their work cut out for them. Not only were there cases of mistaken identity, but a growing number of free blacks were being deliberately kidnapped for sale to slavers. In several cities, reaction was so violent that Federal troops had to be called out to stop riots.

Eventually blood was shed. A Maryland plantation owner named Edward Gorsuch led a party of six into Pennsylvania on the trail of four of his slaves. The escaped slaves had joined a community of blacks living in a little town near Lancaster. When the posse arrived, they discovered that the slaves had barricaded themselves in the house of a black man named William Parker. The posse opened fire on the house. To their surprise, the blacks started firing back. When the pursuers paused to reload, the defenders swarmed out on them, beating and clubbing them. Gorsuch was killed, another was severely wounded, and the rest ran for their lives.

A local paper ran this headline:

CIVIL WAR—THE FIRST BLOW STRUCK!

The nation's attention then shifted to Boston with its well-funded and well-connected Vigilance Committee. The Committee was hard at work helping a fugitive couple from Macon, Georgia, named William and Ellen Craft.

Because Ellen's skin was light enough to pass as white, the couple had devised a bold plan to escape. Ellen would disguise herself as "William Johnson," an invalid gentleman who was accompanied by his body servant (the real William). Unable to read or write, she would keep her right arm in a sling so she would not have to sign any papers.

On the night of December 21, 1848, they blew out the flickering candles in their tiny cabin. "Heavenly Father," they prayed, "please help us like You helped Your people of old to escape from our cruel bondage."

The Lord seemed to be with them. Taking bits of money they had saved, the couple started their terrifying journey north. Before the train to Savannah departed, a white cabinetmaker who had employed William suddenly showed up and began searching each car for them. Just as he reached William's compartment, however, the bell rang. The train was about to leave. The man had to get off.

But there was no breathing easy. Now a friend of their master's sat down in the seat right beside Ellen. Numb with fear, the slave decided to pretend she was deaf. It worked. When the friend discovered the "man" next to him couldn't hear, he spent the rest of the trip to Savannah talking to neighboring passengers about slaves, cotton, and the abolitionists.

In Savannah, the couple booked passage on a steam packet bound for Charleston. During the trip, a crude slave trader harassed Ellen about selling him her body servant. A young army captain intervened and persuaded the trader to leave the "gentleman" alone.

In Charleston, they boarded a steamer for Wilmington, North Carolina. When the black woman asked the steamer's officer to help her sign the ledger, he refused.

"Against regulations," the man said.

Sure enough, the same young captain who had helped before overheard the conversation. He stepped in on her behalf.

"They make it a rule to be very strict at Charleston." The officer shook his head. "If they are not very careful, any abolitionist might take off a lot of valuable niggers."

"I suppose so," Ellen replied, thanking him for his help.

From Wilmington, the invalid and the body servant boarded a train to Fredericksburg and then another steamer to Washington. From there they bought a train ticket to Philadelphia, their final destination. They faced only one more hurdle: changing trains in Baltimore.

"Sir, would you and your manservant please accompany me to the stationmaster's office?" A junior officer of the railroad had approached the couple as they waited to board the Philadelphia train.

"Why?" Ellen replied in a deep voice.

"You may not take a slave out of Baltimore without the stationmaster's permission."

With sinking hearts, the two followed the young man into the office.

"I need proof of ownership." The stationmaster looked up from his desk as he spoke.

"I have our ticket to Philadelphia, sir," she stated matter-of-factly.

"That isn't enough." The man's tone sounded harsher now.

"You have no right to detain us on a technicality," she replied as politely as possible.

The man behind the desk bristled. "Even President Polk can't get on that train 'less I say so."

At that moment, the two runaways felt as if they were about to drown. Within their hearts, they cried out to God. Suddenly, the bell rang. The train was about to depart.

The stationmaster glared at them. Nervously, he ran his knobby fingers through his thin hair. "I don't really know what to do." He paused. "I calculate it's all right." He stood up and turned to the junior officer. "Run and tell the conductor to let this gentleman and his slave pass. He's not well. It's a pity to stop him here."

Ellen thanked him and hobbled out the door and onto the train with William's help. They had made it!

When the two reached Philadelphia, the City of Brotherly Love, Ellen collapsed sobbing into her husband's arms. It was Christmas Day. "Thank God, William, we are safe!" As soon as they reached a boardinghouse, they knelt down and poured out their thanks to God.

They went to Boston, where for two years William worked as a cabinetmaker and Ellen a seamstress. They joined a church and led upstanding lives. They also made a number of friends.

When two slave-hunting agents from Georgia arrived looking for the Crafts, the Boston Vigilance Committee spread the alarm. The Committee posted flyers around town against the agents, and a local magistrate drew up warrants for their arrest, charging them with slander, attempted kidnapping, carrying concealed weapons, smoking on the streets, and cursing. The two agents finally left town.

Down South, the reaction to the new law was very different. The Governor of Georgia called for a state convention to respond to the Compromise. When the delegates met in December they issued the Georgia Platform. "The State of Georgia . . . will and ought to resist . . . to the disruption of every tie that binds her to the Union . . . any act . . . modifying the laws now in force for the recovery of fugitive slaves." Mississippi resolved that the preservation of the Union depended on the "faithful execution of the Fugitive Slave Act." In public referendums in 1851, nearly half of the voters in South Carolina, Georgia, Mississippi, and Alabama went on record that they favored secession from the Union.

It was happening. The South had chosen to remain a part of the United States of America. But everything depended on how sincerely the North intended to enforce the new law. If the Yankees did not honor their word, the South was prepared to leave.

Henry Clay, Daniel Webster, Harriet Beecher Stowe. God had called each of them to a special assignment. Like John

Quincy Adams, Clay and Webster were the last of the grand old guard to defend America as one nation under God. A sadness fell over the country in 1852 when Clay and Webster died. With their passing, America sensed that a great era had drawn to a close. Harriet Beecher Stowe's book so changed the hearts of Northerners against slavery that they would never think of it favorably again.

The wheels of God's pocket watch were turning. But the North would need another 10 years before her resolve against slavery would be a match for the South's resolve in favor of it. The country would also need a strong, godly leader who could usher her through the upheaval to come. In the meantime, God continued to work out His plan . . .

15

KANSAS AND NEBRASKA

Fight the good fight of faith. (1 Timothy 6:12)

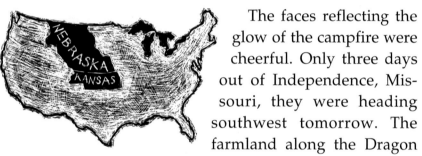

The faces reflecting the glow of the campfire were cheerful. Only three days out of Independence, Missouri, they were heading southwest tomorrow. The farmland along the Dragon River was supposed to be fertile. These families were known as Free-Soilers. They were on their way to Kansas to see that the Kansas Territory came into the Union as a free state.

It was called popular sovereignty. Each territory applying for statehood could decide for itself whether it wanted to be slave or free. In other words, whichever side had the most settlers at the time the state constitution was drawn up would decide how that state would enter the Union. This doctrine lodged yet another wedge between the North and the South.

By the early 1850s, several rail lines reached the Mississippi. The idea of a single railroad line reaching across the entire continent became an urgent topic in Congress. Senator Jefferson Davis of Mississippi wanted such a line to run through the South. With Chicago now the major rail hub of the Midwest, Illinois's Senator Stephen A. Douglas pushed hard for a Northern route.

As chairman of the powerful Committee on Territories, Douglas quickly realized he had to do something. Only one thing stood in his way: A Northern line would have to run through the large uninhabited area known as the Nebraska country. Huge buffalo herds and a few Indian tribes lived here, but pioneers were just now discovering that its prairies were fertile enough to grow such grains as wheat, rye, oats, barley, and corn. Unless the area was organized right away though, the proposed transcontinental rail line would most certainly go south.

Douglas forged what became known as the "Nebraska Bill." This would establish two territories, Nebraska to the north and Kansas to the south. Popular sovereignty would decide the slavery issue. There was one problem: the 1820 Missouri Compromise. Kansas and Nebraska were both north of the 36° 30′ dividing line. According to the Missouri Compromise, slavery was not allowed above this line.

Jefferson Davis and the Southerners in the Senate easily realized that the Missouri Compromise limited their ability to move slaves into both Kansas and Nebraska. They immediately demanded its repeal. Seeing a chance for compromise, Douglas agreed and drew up his Nebraska Bill. The Northern senators were in an uproar. For 30 years this restriction on the Northern expansion of slavery above the dividing line had been carefully observed. Now it was about to be thrown into the dustbin of history.

"The introduction of slavery will retard the prosperity of the state!" an Illinois representative to the House declared as he argued against the bill. "I'm filled with fear for the future of our country," a Yale professor exclaimed. For the first time, businessmen from such centers as Chicago, Cleveland, and Boston met to oppose the bill. And on March 14, the Senate received a petition from 3,050 New England ministers protesting the bill "in the name of Almighty God."

Despite great opposition, however, the Kansas-Nebraska Act passed.

Meanwhile, a situation arose in Boston that propelled formerly neutral Northerners into becoming abolitionists.

A runaway slave named Anthony Burns had been arrested and brought to trial. When his master came to Boston to take Burns back into slavery, Boston's active Vigilance Committee sprang into action. Two nights before his hearing, it held a mass meeting in Faneuil Hall.

"The South is breaking the spirit of Clay's 1850 Compromise," one man argued. "We agreed to it, but look what they're doing!"

"They'll carry slaves to the Rockies if they can!" someone roared.

"If we submit and return Burns to Virginia, then Massachusetts is a conquered state!" another thundered.

At that, the crowd swarmed out of the hall to storm the Federal courthouse. Federal marshals were waiting, loaded rifles in hand. In the end one man was killed and nine jailed.

Flags flew at half mast as throngs of onlookers watched the runaway slave being escorted down the city streets to a ship bound for Virginia. Even the city's church bells tolled.

"When it was all over," one attorney wrote, "I put my face in my hands and wept."

From that moment on, the North ignored the fugitive slave law. Northerners had become convinced that the South intended to extend slavery everywhere.

Looking for a transcontinental railroad, Senator Douglas thought his Nebraska Bill would pull the country together. He could not have been more wrong. Men who had once straddled the slavery fence now jumped down on the antislavery side. By 1854 a new political party had even been formed. This one included antislavery Democrats, Whigs, abolitionists, and Free-Soilers. They called themselves the Republican Party.

The South had long been spoiling for a fight. Now the North was ready for one, too. "We of the North have not sought this struggle, but if it is forced upon us, why, we are ready!"

Once again, the basic issue was slavery, and it was wrenching the nation in two.

16

THE RAIL-SPLITTER

Let us examine and probe our ways,
And let us return to the LORD. (Lamentations 3:40)

The lanky figure tilted his chair back so his feet could find a resting place on the desk. His black coat hung on a peg on the back of the door, and his white shirtsleeves had the cuffs turned back to keep them clean. A tarnished brass spittoon sat beside the desk for anyone who chewed tobacco. And on the shelf behind him was a set of Illinois case law books.

With his hands clasped behind his head, the attorney gazed out the window at the pattern the fall noonday sun made on the old sycamore tree. Anyone glancing in the open door might have thought this country lawyer was daydreaming. But he wasn't. He was thinking. And when Abe Lincoln put his mind to a thing, he was at work.

Abraham Lincoln was born on a small farm in Kentucky in 1809. His pioneer family moved with the frontier—first to Indiana and then to Illinois. His father was a farmer, and his mother was a devout woman who read the Bible to him and his sister; she died when Abe was nine.

The stories about Lincoln's love of reading are true. Many times, he would walk miles just to borrow a book. By the light of the hearth fire, he devoured such books as *Robinson Crusoe, Pilgrim's Progress,* and the plays of William Shakespeare. He also studied the Bible and could quote Scripture at length.

The boy was good with an axe and good with a team of oxen. But he was also good with his mind. By the time he was 21 he had determined he was not going to be a farmer. He worked as a postmaster and a flatboatman down the Mississippi, and he even considered becoming a blacksmith. But it was while he owned a store in New Salem, Illinois, that something happened that changed the course of his life forever.

It was a typical day in this farming community about 20 miles northwest of Springfield. If you walked down the dirt road in the middle of the village, you could hear the barrel maker whistling while he worked. And if you got there early enough, you would see the men arriving to work at the village mill. The few general stores looked like small log cabins with front porches. During the summer months, the shopkeepers had plenty of time on their hands because the farmers were busy with their crops. You would see the clerks sitting on the porches, perched on cane chairs and reading or snoozing.

On this particular day, Abe Lincoln was working in his store when he heard the sound of a horse and wagon outside.

"Whoa!" boomed a deep voice.

The 6'4" shopkeeper ducked through the shop's front door and walked outside.

"Hello, stranger!" he offered in his usual friendly manner.

A family in a covered wagon filled with household goods had stopped right in front of the store. Their two golden-coated horses neighed softly and twitched their ears.

"Hello, sir," the father replied, tying the reins to his seat and jumping down.

Before Lincoln could say another word, the man went on. "Would you be interested in buying an old barrel?"

It turned out the family was migrating West and did not have enough room in their wagon for the barrel.

"Don't know as I really need it," Lincoln replied kindly.

"It doesn't have anything of real value in it," the wife added from her seat atop the wagon. "Just some family books we no longer need."

Lincoln took a deep breath. Always one to help a needy soul, he agreed.

"Will you take a half dollar?"

"Yep," the man hastily replied as he ushered the shop-keeper toward the back of the wagon.

Lincoln's years of splitting logs for rail fences certainly helped him now. After seeing the family on its way, he lugged the heavy barrel inside and stored it in a corner. Sometime later, however, when he found himself with little to do, the shopkeeper decided to rearrange the shop. He happened upon the forgotten barrel.

Hmm, he thought, *wonder what's in this thing?*

With that, Abe dumped its contents onto the shop floor. At the bottom he discovered a complete edition of *Blackstone's Commentaries.* Abe already knew about this book. Written by Sir William Blackstone, an English author and professor, it was the chief source of information about English law.

On a lazy, warm summer afternoon, he began to read. The more he read, the more interested he became. Soon Abraham Lincoln had decided to become a lawyer himself.

Lincoln's great passion was to understand an idea so deeply that he could see where it would lead and how it would affect different people. He could quote Shakespeare or the classics with the best of them, but he preferred to deal in homespun logic and common sense. Once a listener opened his mind to what Lincoln was saying, it was awfully hard to see it any other way.

Lincoln had three other things going for him during his career as a lawyer: compassion, integrity, and honesty. Compassion drew country people to seek out Abraham Lincoln's help. He genuinely cared for people, and they knew it. If they were strapped for cash, he would reduce his fee or give it up altogether. His clients never forgot that.

He was also a man of integrity. He never tried to win more for a client than he felt the client deserved. And if someone wanted his services, he had to convince Lincoln that his cause was just. Moreover, if it turned out that a client had deceived him, Abe would simply quit the case.

On one occasion, Lincoln had presented his client's side to the judge. After he was through, the opposing counsel produced a receipt proving Lincoln's client had lied. Before this attorney had finished talking, Lincoln had left the courtroom and returned to his hotel.

"Go get Mr. Lincoln," the judge ordered.

"Tell the judge that I can't come," Lincoln replied to the clerk. "My hands are dirty, and I came over to clean them."

There were many such stories, and out of them came the nickname that would stick with him forever: "Honest Abe."

By the time he went to Congress in 1847, Lincoln had earned a reputation as one of the most distinguished and successful lawyers in the West. Opposed to the Mexican War, Lincoln had not been nominated for a second term, so he returned to practicing law in his home state of Illinois.

Though out of politics temporarily, he never lost his national perspective. While in Congress, he had wrapped his mind around slavery, examining it carefully. And his position about it had gradually matured. While he did not consider himself an abolitionist, he had become very opposed to the spread of slavery.

When the Kansas-Nebraska Act passed, Lincoln decided to enter politics again. He did so as a Whig, running for the Illinois State Legislature.

Today, Lincoln sat at his desk listening to the cardinal's song in the sycamore tree outside his window. He was thinking about his speech to the Illinois House.

Senator Douglas is coming to push for passage of the bill, he thought. *He's a good speaker.* Abe sat forward and reached for the quill pen on his desk. *My words must be simple and straightforward. The Kansas-Nebraska Act should be repealed.*

On the evening of October 4, the tall, gaunt representative appeared in the House chamber with his speech tucked under his arm. Having spoken the night before, Senator Douglas squared his jaw and tossed his hair back as he glared at Lincoln from the front row. *No matter,* thought the gangly speaker, *I'm ready.*

"Our Founding Fathers raised the banner of freedom on these shores." Lincoln's voice was calm and sure. "For nearly a century, America has given downtrodden multitudes all over the globe cause for hope. Our banner is now faltering.

"The Founding Fathers knew slavery was evil, but they also knew they could not uproot it in a single stroke." Lincoln paused for a brief moment. He passionately wanted these men to understand what he was about to say.

"Our Southern brethren have the constitutional right to own slaves. Would we not feel the same if we were on their side?

"Yet, try as we might, slavery is fundamentally opposed to the very heart of our nation. It violates the spirit of our own Declaration of Independence."

The humidity in the room sent beads of perspiration down the man's long face. He fiddled with his shirt collar and was glad he had not worn a tie.

"As a government created by the consent of the governed, our country has accepted the truth that all men are created equal. This is the very rock on which our nation is founded.

"A man is a man, no matter the color of his skin. A black man is a human being, created by God. The Bible makes this very clear. And our own Declaration affirms it."

Senator Douglas had quick, piercing eyes. Self-confident and sure, Lincoln looked directly at them. "Why do I oppose the Kansas-Nebraska Act? One word. Slavery.

"Supposedly the bill remains indifferent to slavery's spread. I submit otherwise. The bill actually encourages it. And I hate it because it forces so many good men among ourselves into an open war with the fundamental principles of civil liberty. It insists that there is no right principle of action but self-interest."

Lincoln's words seemed to take on a power all by themselves. Turning to the issue of popular sovereignty, he went on.

"Is it right for a territory to decide its status for itself? No. These territories are part of the *national* domain. What occurs there is the concern of every citizen of the United States.

"The bill fails. For example, when will the new settlers in Kansas decide whether it will be free or slave? When there are a thousand of them? Ten thousand? Fifty thousand? And who's to guarantee that popular sovereignty will be decided peaceably? Already, violent border ruffians next door in the slave state of Missouri are taking matters in their own hands. All of us know the contest will—indeed must—lead to bloodshed."

Not a sound but Lincoln's strong voice could be heard. His words made sense. Once again, Lincoln was talking in simple terms everyone could understand. Even the reporters had become so enthralled that they forgot to take notes. This man was speaking the truth, and they knew it.

"Gentlemen, we have a choice," Lincoln concluded. "Either we accept the Spirit of the Declaration or the spirit of Nebraska. Make no mistake about it, slavery is not just a Southern responsibility. It is a *national* responsibility. And the whole world is watching.

"I call for a repeal of the Act and a restoration of the Missouri Compromise. Let us readopt the Declaration of Independence. If we do, we shall not only have saved the Union, but we shall make it forever worthy of the saving!"

The hall jumped to its feet cheering.

Abraham Lincoln had found his national voice—and his calling. With fairness and compassion he had spoken the truth. And anyone with ears to hear it and a heart to accept it knew that it *was* the truth, plain and eternal.

The 45-year-old Illinois Congressman had been right. The furor over Kansas was erupting like a volcano within the territory's borders. Those moving into the territory began carrying rifles for self-defense. The *Kansas Pioneer* encouraged Southerners to come in with rifle, knife, and revolver and get rid of the abolitionists.

When the territorial governor called for an election of a territorial legislature, every able-bodied Missourian who could ride a horse or buckboard crossed into Kansas and voted, as many times as possible. As a result, the newly elected officials favored slavery. In return, the Kansas Free-Soilers elected their own government and even applied to Washington for statehood. Things went from bad to worse. The pro-slavery legislature enacted a law that anyone heard expressing doubts about slavery would find themselves in jail, and anyone caught harboring a fugitive would be hanged.

Men across the South marshaled their forces. They recruited troops to rescue Kansas from the abolitionists. On May 21, 1856, this "Kansas militia" marched on the free-soil town of Lawrence and demanded that it surrender. When it did, abolitionists across the territory vowed revenge.

The Kansas-Nebraska Act's poison seeped back into the United States Congress as well. In March 1855, Congressman Preston Brooks of South Carolina published a letter summing up the Southern mindset: "The admission of Kansas into the Union as a slave State is now a point of honor with the South. . . . It is my deliberate conviction that the fate of the South [will] be decided with the Kansas issue."

Senator Charles Sumner of Massachusetts declared a war on slavery. A prideful man, Sumner had a cruel streak and felt himself above the unwritten rule that members of both houses would address one another in terms befitting their office. His attacks on the personal character of those who opposed him made him the most loathed member of the Senate.

"My colleague from South Carolina can barely even speak properly." The Senator was mocking Andrew Butler who was absent. "He has chosen an ugly mistress, someone he thinks is lovely. That mistress is the harlot, Slavery."

This was too much. Butler's cousin was Congressman Brooks. He decided it was time to break the Congressional code of behavior. That code was for gentlemen, and Sumner was no gentleman. Besides, he had slurred the honor of a senior member of Brooks's family.

On May 22, 1856, Brooks picked up his heavy walking stick and strode into the Senate chamber. An unsuspecting Sumner sat at his desk mulling over a speech.

"Sir, I have read your speech twice," Brooks announced, "and you have defamed our family's name!"

With that the angry South Carolinian struck the Senator on his head and shoulders, pounding him over and over. The thick cane split into smaller and smaller pieces as he beat the man senseless to the floor.

William Cullen Bryant of the New York *Evening Post* summed up the situation: "Violence has now found its way into the Senate chamber. Violence lies in wait on all the navigable rivers and all the railways of Missouri, to obstruct those who pass from the Free States into Kansas. Violence overhangs the frontiers of that Territory like a stormcloud charged with hail and lightning."

The news of the caning of Sumner clicked across the telegraph wires stretching to Kansas. As it reached the frontier, it set off a lightning storm of violence even greater than before.

It was just the beginning . . .

17

1857

The word of God is not imprisoned.
(2 Timothy 2:9)

 Abraham Lincoln and Stephen A. Douglas were giants in leadership. But now a man of considerably less character was about to step to center stage.

In the fall of 1856, James Buchanan was elected President. The weak-chinned, portly man had served as Secretary of State under President Polk. Since both Northerners and Southerners still belonged to the Democratic Party, the results of this election represented the fading hope that the Union could still be preserved. Yet many Northerners looked on the Pennsylvania native as a man with Southern principles. This President believed in popular sovereignty and thought Kansas should decide for itself about slavery.

Surprisingly, the young Republican party won most of the North and almost took Buchanan's home state. Like a heavy weight on one end of a tilting seesaw, the issue of slavery was beginning to decide who would win national elections. To take the White House in 1860, four years from now, all the Republicans had to do was hold onto the states they already had and pick up Pennsylvania and another state such as Illinois.

Buchanan was inaugurated on March 4, 1857. Two days after his inauguration, something very important occurred. The United States Supreme Court issued its verdict in the case of Dred Scott—a decision that propelled the nation to the brink of war.

Dred Scott was an elderly black slave owned by an Army surgeon named John Emerson. Dr. Emerson lived in Missouri, a slave state. When the doctor was transferred to the free state of Illinois in 1834, he took his slave with him. Two years later he went to the Wisconsin Territory, where slavery was also outlawed. But eventually he and Scott returned to Missouri, where Emerson died in 1843.

Three years after this, some local antislavery lawyers helped Scott sue the doctor's widow for his freedom. His lawyers argued that the years the slave had spent in the free states of Illinois and Wisconsin had made him a free man.

In his written opinion, Chief Justice Roger Taney reviewed the supreme law of the land. The Constitution defined a slave as property, and the Fifth Amendment guaranteed that no one should "be deprived of life, liberty or property without due process of law."

Dred Scott did not even have the right to sue, wrote Taney. Blacks were property and therefore not U.S. citizens. Slaveholders had a constitutional right to take their property with them wherever they went.

Taney could have stopped there, but he didn't. He took this opportunity to issue an opinion about the Missouri Compromise of 1820. Repealed in 1854 through the Kansas-Nebraska Bill, the constitutionality of the Missouri Compromise had been a topic of national debate ever since. Taney wanted to put the issue to rest.

Because slaves are property, he said, any law forbidding the spread of slavery is unconstitutional. Such a law violates a slave owner's constitutional right to own property.

In other words, Congress could not prohibit slavery *anywhere!*

Northern newspapers instantly condemned the decision. "Wherever our flag floats, it is the flag of slavery," proclaimed the New York *Post.* "The Decision of the Supreme Court Is the Moral Assassination of a Race and Cannot Be Obeyed," headlined the *Independent.* No longer could a Northerner remain neutral. The Slave States were going to take over!

One more hand was dealt before 1857 closed, and it had to do with Kansas.

Having applied for statehood, the Territory of Kansas held a constitutional convention in the territorial capital of Lecompton. Unfortunately, those who favored slavery had illegally drawn the county boundaries so the districts would include a majority of slaveholders. When the Free-Soilers refused to vote in the unfair election, the proslavery forces won and passed a constitution that included slavery.

President Buchanan now made the greatest blunder of his weak administration. He urged Congress to accept the Lecompton constitution. But hadn't he advocated popular sovereignty and wasn't this election illegal?

Many Democrats, including Senator Douglas from Illinois, realized the President had jumped ship—he clearly favored the South. As a result, the Democratic party split. The only remaining political instrument holding the North and South together had been destroyed.

Due to Douglas's influence, Congress sent the constitution back to Kansas without approving it. It was eventually defeated, so Kansas could come in free.

However, the damage had been done. The South controlled the Federal Government. The Supreme Court had voted in favor of the South. The Executive was a Southern sympathizer, and half of Congress was Southern. The North was just waiting for the South to carve Texas into five slave states.

Equally fearful, the South looked ahead at Oregon and Montana as well as Kansas and Nebraska coming in as free states. The North's booming industrial economy and the huge numbers of immigrants only made matters worse. What would the South do?

Like a locomotive at full throttle, the country was barreling around the sharp curve toward an unseen precipice. If Americans did not resolve the issue of slavery, there would be a terrible disaster.

Yet, with God nothing is impossible. And God Himself was about to give America one last opportunity to avoid His judgment. Would she listen?

18

"STAND UP, STAND UP FOR JESUS"

*[If] My people who are called by My name humble
themselves and pray . . . and turn from their wicked
ways, then I will . . . heal their land.
(2 Chronicles 7:14)*

The tall man knelt on the floor, listening to the silence. Although he could hear the muffled sounds of New York City far below, he heard only the slow *tick . . . tock* of the wall clock here on the third floor. Its hands read 12:14. Jeremiah Lanphier watched a particle of dust suspended in a shaft of noonday sun through the south window. Somehow he would keep waiting.

In 1857 New York City was changing as rapidly as the rest of America. Its downtown area was becoming more industrialized, and many people were moving uptown. As a result, the membership in many of the downtown churches was dwindling. The churches began looking for ways to draw new congregations from among the many immigrants. The old North Dutch Church on Fulton Street had recently hired Lanphier as a full-time lay evangelist to reach them.

The task was a huge one. As the summer passed, however, few responded to the evangelist's personal calls or the pamphlets he was giving out. But Jeremiah was a man of prayer; he knew God would somehow show him the way.

One day, while walking along a city street, he had a strange idea. Why not offer an hour of prayer, from 12:00 to 1:00? Businessmen could stop by during their lunch time, even if only for five or ten minutes. The more Jeremiah thought about it, the more excited he became.

Today was the right day, September 23, 1857. The meeting was to have started at noon. Doubts rushed into his mind like hornets. Had he done everything? He had printed and passed out handbills telling where and when this first businessmen's prayer meeting would take place. The wall clock now struck 12:30. Jeremiah knelt on the floor alone. God had called him to this; he would stay.

Then, ever so quietly the downstairs door creaked open. Jeremiah heard steps on the stairs. A stranger opened the door, walked into the room, and without a word, knelt beside Jeremiah.

Another came, and another. By 1:00 there were 6. The following week there were 20. The week after that there were 40. By October 8, so many men were praying that Jeremiah had to move the meeting to a larger room on the second floor. By the fourth Wednesday there were over a hundred. Jeremiah later wrote that they were seeking Christ and asking what they needed to do to be saved.

As men were blessed, they encouraged friends to join them. And as Jeremiah had hoped, the meetings drew men from all classes of society and all trades. Draymen would tie up their teams, slip in for a few minutes, then leave. Shop foremen would mention the meetings to their workers. Hotels would recommend them to their guests.

Jeremiah's purpose for the meetings was prayer, pure and simple. And his rules were strict. The meetings would begin promptly at noon. At five minutes to 1:00 the leader would announce a closing hymn and benediction, and the meeting was over.

These meetings became known as the "Fulton Street Meetings." Before long, all three of the church's meeting rooms were filled. The John Street Methodist Church around the corner opened to handle the overflow. Other churches followed, many opening at noon, others opening before work. Soon there was such a need for places to pray that even the police and fire stations opened their doors for prayer!

One night Henry Ward Beecher, the son of Lyman Beecher, spoke on Chambers Street. He told this true story.

"A buyer came here from Albany and called on a merchant to buy goods. At twelve o'clock, the New York merchant looked at his watch.

"'I need to be excused,' the seller said plainly.

"'But we're not through. I'd like to finish our business.' The buyer was clearly dismayed.

"The merchant shook his head. 'I'm sorry, but I must attend the prayer meeting.'

"'Can't you pray in the morning or at night?' The buyer's voice was agitated.

"The New Yorker closed his ledger. 'Going to these meetings is more important to me than selling my whole stock of goods,' the merchant replied. 'Why don't you come with me? It only lasts an hour.'

165

"After some persuading, the Albany visitor agreed. He went into the meeting and came out a converted man. When he returned home, he immediately started his own prayer meetings, and the people have been blessed."

Beecher's words affected his listeners greatly. That day, many men accepted Christ.

Today the word *revival* has been so overused that it is almost worthless. In the true meaning of the word, revival was a nationwide, earthshaking event. It was an act of God reaching down and changing the lives of men and societies. And it was beginning to happen again in America.

Interestingly enough, New York City was not the only place such prayer meetings were taking place that summer of 1857. Independent of one another, businessmen in other cities had started to meet and pray, too. The Holy Spirit was drawing them together. This new "awakening" was truly a sovereign act of God.

America had experienced such revivals before. The first was the Great Awakening beginning in the mid–1730s. Through this, many of the people in the Colonies had given their lives to Christ. Without that spiritual preparation, America would never have survived its struggle for independence.

The next revival came at the dawn of the 19th century, and it happened in places as different as frontier camp meetings and the campus of Yale College. This Second Great Awakening ebbed and flowed but never really died away. Lane Seminary and Theodore Dwight Weld were a part of it.

Several things were different about this new wave of the revival, though. First, this one was quieter. Gone were the loud preachings of the frontier camp meetings; this time the focus was prayer. Second, it was carried forth by laypeople and church members rather than Methodist circuit riders or ministers.

Revival was in the New England air. Even the newspapers and colleges were becoming centers of revival. In 1857 Boston's *Watchman and Reflector* decided to focus its publication on a campaign to promote spiritual awakening. Soon its news columns were filled with reports of exciting efforts to start revivals across New England. Such colleges as Amherst, Williams, and Yale saw scores of conversions. And the Young Men's Christian Association (YMCA), begun in Boston in 1851, opened its doors in other cities.

The Holy Spirit was doing an extraordinary work, even on the high seas. At one point, a ship arrived in New York Harbor with its captain and crew of 29 men having been converted right in the middle of the Atlantic Ocean! Soon after that, five other ships sailed in, each with captains and crews who had given their lives to Christ. Before long, seamen with shore leave were no longer looking for a place to gamble and drink; they were seeking places to worship.

A religious periodical in New York City reported 50,000 conversions in the city during the first five months of 1858. God was reaching down and touching the lives of His people. For many years the faithful had been praying for just such a revival. And God was keeping His promise in 2 Chronicles 7:14. His people, the ones called by His name, *were* praying and seeking His face and turning from their wicked ways.

And He was hearing their prayers and was pouring out His Spirit upon all flesh.

The revival was not confined to New England's borders, however. During early January 1858, Presbyterians reported unusual awakenings in Memphis, Cleveland, and Nashville. Baptists announced revival not only in their New England churches but also in Pennsylvania and the western states. The Methodists documented similar experiences in cities from New York to Illinois. Philadelphia, Albany, Boston, Cincinnati—all reported outbreaks of prayer meetings.

Before long, all denominations and all the states in the Union were heard from.

In Chicago, a shoe salesman from Boston was astonished when the merchant he was calling on looked at his watch and said, "I must go to my prayer meeting now." The salesman went with him.

"I go to meeting every night," he later wrote his mother. "Oh, how I enjoy it! It seems as if God were here Himself. O Mother, pray for me! Pray that His work may go on till every knee is bowed!"

Soon Dwight L. Moody would turn in his shoe kit and go into full-time evangelism. Today the Moody Bible Institute in Chicago trains pastors, missionaries, and lay leaders, operates 11 radio stations, and publishes Christian books and magazines.

In February of 1858, the Holy Spirit led Jeremiah Lanphier to call on James Gordon Bennett, editor of the powerful New York *Herald*.

The pleasant-faced, middle-aged Lanphier sat in the busy newspaper office. The sounds of clicking typesetting equipment and rustling papers filled his ears. Men with visors and rolled-up sleeves leaned over huge desks racked with type. Jeremiah wasn't sure he liked the smell of the ink.

Before long, Mr. Bennett opened the door of his office. "Come in, won't you?"

"Mr. Bennett, I'll get right to the point." The evangelist took off his cap when he sat down. "There is something very big happening in our city, and you need to know about it."

The editor had already walked behind the desk.

"There's a revival, sir," Jeremiah fingered his hat, "a spiritual renewal. It covers all denominations, and it's growing. Men and women are giving their lives to Christ."

Bennett didn't believe Jeremiah at first, but he sent a reporter down to Fulton Street anyway. When the editor read the man's copy, he realized just how big a story he was sitting on. The headline read: "The Prayer Revival."

Bennett's archrival was Horace Greeley, editor of the New York *Tribune.* Not to be outdone, Greeley sent his own reporters to write stories, too. They were converted. By April, Greeley devoted an entire issue of his weekly edition to the revival.

These two New York newspapers held more influence than any other dailies in the country. When they gave front-page attention to something, it became news everywhere. Soon readers across the country were learning about the revival. And editors were discovering that the same thing was happening in their own backyards. The revival was a huge event, now being covered by secular periodicals.

In Philadelphia, reporters from the Philadelphia *Press* attended a midday meeting in Jayne's Hall. "There were three thousand persons," they wrote, "the largest meeting ever convened in our country for the simple purpose of prayer to God."

The leadership of these meetings fell on a young evangelical Episcopal minister, Dudley Tyng. "Ye that are men . . . serve the Lord," Tyng preached to a packed hall one Sunday morning in March. More than 1,000 men confessed Christ that day.

By April, all the big halls in Philadelphia could not hold the praying people. Thirty-five firehouses opened their doors. As a result, 1,500 burly rough firemen got converted, too.

A few days after his sermon, Tyng got his arm caught and mangled in a piece of farm machinery. The arm could not be saved. He did not recover from the amputation. He lay dying in the hospital with his friend, George Duffield, at his side.

"Tell the men at Jayne's Hall to stand up for Jesus." Tyng's weak voice was soft.

"I will," Duffield nodded sadly.

He kept his word. Today, Duffield's hymn is the standard for prayer revivals everywhere:

> Stand up, stand up for Jesus,
> ye soldiers of the Cross;
> lift high His royal banner,
> it must not suffer loss:
> From victory unto victory
> His army shall He lead,
> till every foe is vanquished,
> and Christ is Lord indeed.

Other hymns became favorites too: "Jesus Loves Me" and "He Leadeth Me" came out of the Philadelphia revival. "Just As I Am" and "What a Friend We Have in Jesus" are still sung today.

Clearly, the Holy Spirit was spiritually preparing His people in the North for the coming ordeal. But what about the

South? Wouldn't He do the same for His people in the South, black and white? The answer was yes.

J. M. C. Breaker was a black Baptist pastor in Beaufort, South Carolina. By the end of 1857, he had baptized 565 new members that year, a record for his church. That brought his membership up to 3,511, which made his church probably the largest in North America.

In 1858 the nationwide membership in the Methodist Church more than tripled. That same year, the Episcopalians in Kentucky recorded a 22 percent increase in enrollment. By spring Tennessee had experienced revival in 40 towns, while Mississippi documented similar happenings.

In Charleston, the Reverend John L. Girardeau began nightly prayer meetings to seek an outpouring of the Holy Spirit. Night after night, he led his flock in prayer. Gradually his church pews filled up.

One evening, Dr. Girardeau felt something like a bolt of electricity shoot through his body. For a while he could not speak. Finally he was able to utter a few words.

"The Holy Spirit has come. We will begin preaching tomorrow evening."

The pastor ended the service. But no one left. Every single person remained seated. It didn't take long for the pastor to realize what was happening. The Holy Spirit had not only come to him; He had also come to the people!

"Accept Jesus. The Holy Spirit is here," he told them.

Before long, he could hear sobbing. It sounded like softly falling rain. While some members wept, others rejoiced. The service did not end until midnight.

With 1,000 to 2,000 people attending each night, the Charleston meetings continued for eight weeks. Historians calculate that at one point, 50,000 people were accepting Christ *each week* across the nation. What was God doing? Dr. Girardeau understood. The revival was "the Lord's mercy in gathering His elect for the great war that will soon sweep so many into eternity," he wrote.

Before the War for Independence, the Lord had spiritually prepared the nation to go through the refining fire to come. He was doing the same thing again. Now, He was bringing one more person onto the center of the stage. This man would become one of the greatest of America's statesmen.

19

A HOUSE DIVIDED

Any kingdom divided against itself is laid waste; and
any city or house divided against itself shall not stand.
(Matthew 12:25)

The place was Springfield, Illinois. The time was the middle of June 1858.

The smell of leather-bound books filled the State House library. Twelve men sat quietly around a table. They were listening to a tall, thoughtful-looking man with hollow cheeks and dark hair. The Republican candidate for the United States Senate was asking his trusted advisors their opinion of his acceptance speech.

It focused on the issue of slavery.

"A house divided against itself cannot stand." Abraham Lincoln spoke straight from the heart. "I believe this government cannot endure permanently, half slave and half free."

Some of the men were dismayed. It was one thing to privately believe this but quite another to put it on record.

Lincoln went on. "I do not expect the Union to be dissolved. I do not expect the house to fall. But I *do* expect it will cease to be divided. It will become all one thing, or all the other."

A few shifted uncomfortably in their seats.

"Either the opponents of slavery will arrest the further spread of it, or its advocates will push it forward until it shall become lawful in all the states."

He concluded. "Well, what do you think?" The prairie lawyer looked at his friends.

"It's too radical, Abe," one man declared. "You've gone too far with that 'house divided' business."

Lincoln took a deep breath. A negative spell seemed to have been cast on the meeting.

"I would rather be defeated with this expression *in* the speech, than to win without it," he replied truthfully.

"Lincoln," Billy Herndon, his former law partner spoke up, "deliver that speech as read, and it will make you President!"

He smiled as he pulled down the too-short sleeves on his black dress coat. "Gentlemen," he said, "the time has come when these sentiments should be uttered. If I go down because of this speech, then let me go down linked to the truth."

The candidate entered the hall to thunderous applause. During his speech, the crowd frequently interrupted him with wild cheering. When he finished, the final approval was deafening. Lincoln had taken a public stand on slavery and had taken the Republican party with him.

Lincoln's opponent for the U.S. Senate seat was Senator Stephen A. Douglas, whose six-year term in Washington was expiring. When the Democrat learned about Lincoln's acceptance speech, Douglas's advisors assured him he had nothing to worry about. After all, he was an 11-year veteran of the Senate and a superb politician. Besides, who was this Lincoln? A cracker-barrel lawyer in ill-fitting clothes who looked more like a scarecrow than a man. No one had ever heard of him. Douglas would crush him like an ant.

But the Senator was not so sure. He had heard Lincoln in Springfield. He had seen the charisma of this too tall, too thin bumpkin whose voice cracked when he talked. This man could think—deeply and carefully.

"I shall have my hands full," the square-jawed Douglas cautioned his handlers. "He is the strong man of his party—full of wit, facts, dates—and he is the best stump speaker in the West. He is as honest as he is shrewd, and if I beat him, my victory will be hardly won."

Douglas and Lincoln hit the campaign trail. At one point, Lincoln wrote his opponent, suggesting a series of debates in different parts of Illinois. These would be regulated discussions of various issues between the two of them. Douglas accepted.

Agreement was reached. There would be seven debates, two in northern Illinois (Republican country), two in the south (Douglas country), and three in the middle (up for grabs). The first would be in Ottawa, in the middle of the state, on August 21; the last, in the southwest at Alton on October 15. Each debate would last three hours.

Interest ran high. The biggest newspapers sent their best reporters to cover the debates. The Chicago *Tribune,* whose publisher, Joseph Medill, was a friend of Lincoln's, sent a reporter who knew shorthand. For the first time in history, the entire country would read every word.

In 1858 Ottawa was a tree-shaded, sleepy little town on the Illinois River, about 75 miles southwest of Chicago. Surrounded by fields of ripening corn, the town had a population of 6,000. By the morning of August 21, the townspeople had whitewashed their fences, tacked up large flags on their porches, and prepared their food baskets. Companies of militia in parade-dress uniforms marched down the street as children shouted, horses neighed, and dogs barked.

All morning long, special trains and boats had been arriving from Chicago. In fact, hundreds of carriages, buckboards, and buggies choked the road with dust. By early afternoon, the town's population had swollen to nearly 20,000, an enormous crowd for that part of the state. Drums banged, fifes trilled, and all of Ottawa throbbed with excitement.

Shortly before one o'clock, a great cheer arose from the Democrats. Senator Douglas and his beautiful new wife were approaching in a four-horse carriage on the La Salle Road. A cavalcade of horsemen galloped out of town, banners flying, to escort him in. As the carriage came into view, a band struck up. Dressed in a dazzling white linen suit and black patent-leather shoes, Douglas waved to his fans as he emerged from the carriage. With his broad-brimmed fedora, he looked magnificent.

Not to be outdone, the Republicans greeted their man at the train station and placed him in a carriage adorned with evergreens. In contrast to Douglas, Lincoln wore a black dress coat with sleeves that were too short, a battered stovepipe hat, and black trousers that ended well before they met his shoes. As one reporter wrote, he was a Kentucky type, tall, slender, and awkward.

The crowd was so tightly packed, it took half an hour to get the two speakers the final hundred yards to the platform. Finally, everything was ready, and the first debate began.

"Everyone knows Douglas," scribbled the New York *Evening Post*'s reporter, "a short, burly man with a large round head, heavy hair, and dark complexion."

From the start, Douglas dug hard and deep. He attacked Lincoln personally. He accused him of creating an abolition party under the name of Republicans. And he challenged Lincoln to tell the crowd exactly where he stood on the original Republican platform issued in Springfield four years before.

"I have here a draft of that platform," Douglas stated. "Does my opponent truly favor a repeal of the Fugitive Slave Act?" The Senator smirked when he asked this question. If Lincoln answered yes, he would lose the support of the South; if he answered no, the North would be upset.

"Does he believe the country should acquire new territory only if slavery is prohibited there?" A look of satisfaction crossed the speaker's square jaw. The proslavery people wouldn't like this one a bit.

Under the rules, Lincoln could not immediately reply. As he listened, wrinkles appeared on his brow. This afternoon, the man whose genius was known statewide did not seem sure of himself at all.

Douglas pounced on Lincoln's "House Divided" speech next.

"It's a declaration of war against the slaveholding South!" the well-dressed, portly man argued with passion. "The country has endured half slave and half free for 70 years. Why should it not continue to exist with these institutions that have benefited it so long?"

The crowd cheered.

"I don't question Mr. Lincoln's belief that the Negro was made his equal and is his brother."

Loud laughter ripped through the large crowd.

"But *my* stand is clear," he proclaimed with his hand in the air. "I am personally opposed to Negro citizenship in every form. I do not regard the Negro as my equal, and positively deny that he is my brother.

"However, the decision about the Negro's status does not—and should not—rest in my hands. It lies solely with our individual states. They should decide for themselves. Popular sovereignty is the true democratic spirit!"

Lincoln spoke next.

"The natural right of the Negro to life, liberty, and the pursuit of happiness must be respected." The words coming out of his mouth sounded almost timid.

Instead of rebutting Douglas's specific charges about the Republican platform, Lincoln merely pointed out that he had not been present at the party's founding convention. After a few more points, he read from the text of a speech he had given earlier in Peoria, Illinois. He sat down long before the time expired.

From the looks of things, Senator Douglas had clearly won this contest. But then something happened that changed people's opinions.

After the Ottawa debate, the reporter for the Chicago *Tribune* decided to look into Douglas's allegations about the Republican platform and Lincoln's connections to it. To his surprise, none of Douglas's points were even contained in the party's original platform. To form his accusations the Senator had used a list made at another meeting, an abolitionist meeting, whose members Lincoln did not even know. Like a green garter snake slithering between the blades of tall summer grass, Douglas had tried to sneak this trickery by.

Today, politicians pull this kind of dirty trick all the time. In 1858 however, it was front-page news. Douglas had flat-out lied. And he had gotten caught. Editorials condemning the Senator's action were transmitted across telegraph wires around the country.

The next stop at Freeport loomed in the distance like a mountain range. Lincoln shook off his despair. The Illinois lawyer had to pull himself up by his suspenders and drive on. The candidate decided he would not battle his opponent by attacking him for his deception. He would do it with the truth.

Douglas was playing his strongest card: popular sovereignty. But it contained a fatal flaw: Just the year before, the Supreme Court had ruled popular sovereignty null and void in the Dred Scott decision. And Douglas had supported this decision. So, how could the people of a territory refuse incoming slaves, if the Supreme Court said a man could take his property anywhere?

It was a loaded question, and Lincoln knew it. If Douglas declared that the Court's decision *was* supreme, agreeing that a man could take his slaves as property anywhere, he would lose the Illinois election. If he didn't, suggesting a man could not take slaves anywhere as property, he might win Illinois, but he'd lose any Southern support—and with it, any hope of the Presidency in 1860.

This time, the man with the high forehead and awkward gait was a different man than he had been in Ottawa. This time, his face had the determination of a lion on the prowl.

First, he responded to the Senator's questions in Ottawa.

"I believe the South is entitled to the Fugitive Slave Act, and I have not asked for its repeal," he began confidently.

"And yes, I am pledged to prohibit slavery in all Federal territories. However, any decision I might make about acquiring a new territory would depend on whether it would aggravate the slavery question among ourselves."

Lincoln's deep-set eyes narrowed. He came in for the kill. "The question as I see it is this: Can the people of a United States territory lawfully exclude slavery before forming a state constitution?"

A skilled debater, the Senator immediately saw the pit his adversary was digging. If Douglas did not back his popular sovereignty stand, he would lose his Senate seat. But if he denied the Court's Dred Scott decision making slaves a man's property wherever he traveled with them, he would lose his Southern support for the Presidency. He decided to skirt the issue.

"While the Supreme Court's ruling is the law of the land, a territory could pass '*unfriendly* legislation' if it wanted to," Douglas argued expertly. "So a community could still ban slavery. No matter what the Supreme Court may say, the *right* of the people to make a territory slave or free is perfect and complete."

Lincoln smiled. Douglas may have gotten around the issue, but Lincoln had accomplished what he intended. Douglas's stand became known as his Freeport Doctrine: Slavery could be kept out of the territories, if the people there did not want it and made local laws against it.

For the next two months, two different railroad cars whistled through the Illinois countryside carrying the debaters. They reached their fifth stop at Galesburg on October 7. The cold gray day did not keep some 20,000 people from attending. Shivering to the bone in the hard wind, they listened.

"Freedom of choice is the cornerstone of American democracy!" Senator Douglas declared.

Lincoln was not outdone. "This is true," he countered swiftly. "But there is a higher law. A man's freedom of choice ceases the moment that choice affects another man's freedom."

In Quincy, Lincoln placed his scarred black satchel and umbrella next to his chair before speaking. He towered over his opponent, now as much in his words as in his stature.

"Judge Douglas says that whoever wants slaves has a right to have them. He is perfectly logical, if there is nothing wrong in the institution." He paused. "But if slavery is wrong, how can he say that someone has a right to do what is wrong?"

Lincoln had been waiting for this moment. At last, he had thrust his lance into the heart of Douglas's position on popular sovereignty: If a people can determine whether they want something, then they have the right to *anything* they want, even if it's wrong.

The heart of Lincoln's argument was that self-government requires constant vigilance to preserve and protect the God-given rights of *all* the people. Inspired by the Bible itself, the Declaration of Independence defines these rights. The prairie lawyer knew that without a vibrant Christian faith in the hearts of the people, there is nothing to control the evil passions. Eventually the people will no longer want to do the right thing.

His words touched the hearts of his listeners that day in Quincy, and readers around the country responded as well. Before the debates, hardly anyone outside of Illinois had heard of "Honest Abe." Now they were reading his speeches, word for word, all over the country.

"Who is this man who is replying to Douglas in your state?" a man from the East wrote the editor of the Chicago *Tribune.*

"Do you realize that no greater speeches have been made on public questions in the history of our country?"

The final debate was in Alton, where the abolitionist editor Elijah Lovejoy had been murdered by an angry mob 21 years before.

Dressed in a fine blue wool suit, Douglas spoke first. The buttons on his shiny brocade vest poked out on his broad chest. "I will never abandon the principle of popular sovereignty," he maintained staunchly. "I will defend it and follow it wherever it leads."

"It is the eternal struggle between these two principles—right and wrong," Lincoln maintained earnestly. "All of our debates boil down to one thing: whether slavery is right or wrong. My opponent refuses to treat it as wrong. I will never be able to treat it as right.

"The only rock upon which man's political salvation is built is his sense of morals. No man can rightfully achieve freedom for himself, in the presence of a just God, if he denies to any other man, of whatever race or nation, the right to freedom."

In the end, Senator Douglas was reelected. When Lincoln received word back in his law office the evening of the election, he turned up the lamp and penned a letter to a friend.

"I am glad I made the late race," he wrote. "It gave me a hearing on the great question of the age, which I could have had in no other way. And though I shall be forgotten, I believe I have made some marks which will tell of the cause of civil liberty long after I have gone."

But this man did not sink from view. Across America, Abraham Lincoln's name was now ringing the bell against slavery.

He had become the chief spokesman of the antislavery cause and the leader in the army of freedom.

God still had plans for Lincoln, and He would soon place him squarely where He wanted him. But it wasn't quite time yet. Something sinister was lurking like a wild jackal just around the next bend.

20

STORM WARNINGS

*Vengeance is Mine. . . . For the day of their calamity
is near, And the impending things are hastening upon
them. (Deuteronomy 32:35)*

The white-bearded figure driving the wagon turned to check on his troop. Behind him 21 men marched silently in a double column, each with a rifle and pistols. The only sound was the creaking of the wagon's wheels.

It began to drizzle, and John Brown drew his long coat closer about him. He smiled. The rain would keep people indoors on this night, and their dogs, which might bark, under cover. This would make it easier to move into Harpers Ferry. The Provisional Army of the United States, as Brown had named it, was on the march.

Located at the junction of the Potomac and Shenandoah Rivers, Harpers Ferry was a busy little town with nearly 1,800 inhabitants. Many of the locals worked in the United States Rifle Factory with its several million dollars' worth of arms and munitions. Brown and his militia were headed there on this misty night of October 16, 1859.

As the wagon rolled over a rock in the road, the load under the canvas behind the captain shifted. He had enough weapons for this first phase at least: 50 rifles and 1,000 blades attached to the end of long poles. But this wasn't enough for the war that was about to take place. To begin his military campaign to free the slaves, Brown needed the rifles and ammunition stored in the arsenal at Harpers Ferry.

It was a simple, clear-cut plan, and it couldn't fail. Once they had taken the armory, they would have the ammunition necessary to stage the uprising. When word got out, antislavery men from all over nearby Pennsylvania, Maryland, and western Virginia would certainly rally to the cause. As soon as the slaves heard that a deliverer had finally arrived, they would flock to him, too.

From his youth, Brown had hated slavery. Since 1855 he and his sons had used their Sharps rifles to keep Kansas free. He would not let anything—or anyone—stand in his way. He had organized a small army and installed himself as their captain.

As the wagon jostled along, the captain remembered with satisfaction one fateful night in Kansas. Claiming to be God's avenging angel, he had dragged five slavery sympathizers out in their nightshirts and split open their skulls like melons.

No, he thought, he wasn't a violent man. But he was absolutely convinced that God had called him to this, and he would give his life if he had to. And he knew exactly what to do. Soon this small band would become a mighty army of freemen heading south through the Appalachian Mountains to free the slaves. Slavery was doomed forever.

The plan was so foolproof that Brown felt he didn't need an escape plan. Never mind that he had not alerted sympathetic whites or slaves in the local area of his proposed raid. Never mind that Harpers Ferry was a perfect trap, surrounded by mountains and rivers. Never mind that a superior force could get there quickly by rail and seal off the escape route. He pursed his thin lips and cocked his head to one side. This plan could not fail.

The bridge wasn't far away. As the road began to descend to the river, Brown drew up the horse and raised his right hand. The column behind him stopped, then gathered round the wagon. He pointed to the lights of the town below and silently waved his hand forward.

Two men detached themselves to cut the telegraph wires. Without a word, the rest ran forward to the wagon-and-railroad bridge. There they seized the surprised watchman. Two of the men remained behind as guards, while the others hurried on to secure the second bridge. Located just a half mile up the Shenandoah, the rifle works was an easy target. The men rushed up there and took possession.

Brown was pleased. The first phase of the attack was now complete. It was still two hours before midnight, and the armory was already in their hands.

"Now, to Colonel Washington's!" the tight-lipped leader ordered. Six of his men headed into Virginia toward the home of a prominent slaveholder, Colonel Lewis W. Washington, great-grandnephew of George Washington. Within a few hours, the band had kidnapped Colonel Washington and freed four of his slaves.

All that was left was to let the country know what they had done. Brown planned to accomplish this through the midnight mail express from Wheeling to Baltimore. Due at the Harpers Ferry station at one o'clock, it arrived right on schedule.

"What's that?" As the train was leaving the town, the engineer noticed something blocking the track ahead at the bridge. He stopped the train and hopped out. Out of nowhere, the sound of a nearby rifle deafened his ears. The frightened man dashed back to the cab, threw the big drivers into reverse, and backed the train into the station.

Shepherd Hayward, the station's baggagemaster, decided to find out what was going on.

Where's the watchman? the free black wondered as he walked down the track toward the bridge.

"Halt!" someone shouted.

Hayward had never heard this word before, so he didn't know what it meant. It didn't sound like the voice of a friend, though. When the unsuspecting man hurried forward, another shot rang out, hitting him in his stomach. Twelve hours later, he died, his body still lying by the tracks where he had been shot. The first blood drawn by the sword of vengeance that had come to free all blacks was the blood of a black man who was already free.

At five in the morning, Brown released the train, knowing that word would now spread far and wide. The beady-eyed captain assumed the conductor would relay his invitation to all men, black and white, to join him. Instead, the conductor telegraphed that a Negro revolt was occurring at Harpers Ferry.

By early morning, the shooting and commotion at the arsenal and train station had awakened the town. Soon riders were alerting the countryside, and farmers from the surrounding area were snatching up their shotguns or squirrel rifles and heading for the Ferry. However, they weren't planning to join anything; they were going to protect the town.

Captain Brown had not anticipated that raw farmers could move so quickly, nor had he realized that the men who lived in Virginia's Blue Ridge Mountains were among the best shots in the country.

Where are my reinforcements? Brown asked himself inside the brick firehouse where he had set up headquarters. The train left six hours ago. The whole countryside should know by now.

Back in the nation's capital, President Buchanan immediately dispatched a detachment of Marines under the command of Lieutenant Colonel Robert E. Lee of the Second Cavalry. Lieutenant James Ewell Brown Stuart went with him. They arrived by train at midnight.

Early the next morning, Lee turned to Stuart. "Lieutenant Stuart, you carry this note to Brown containing the terms of the surrender," the senior officer instructed. "If he rejects them, get out of the way and signal the attack."

Stuart took the note, saluted, and started walking slowly toward the firehouse. Lee thought about what courage it took to do this; Stuart could be shot in an instant.

The door cracked open, and John Brown took the note.

"I'm the one dictating the terms!" he growled through yellowed teeth. "I have a number of hostages now. I'll give them up but only if you guarantee us safe passage to the bridge and—"

Stuart shook his head.

Brown snarled, "We soldiers are not afraid of death. I would as leave die by a bullet as on the gallows."

With a sigh, Stuart leaped aside, took off his cap, and used it to wave the Marines forward. That was the signal. With a yell, they charged. Using a heavy ladder, they rammed through the oak planks of the door and poured in the opening. Both sides opened fire at point-blank range. Within minutes, it was over. John Brown was captured beside the bodies of two of his sons, one dying, one dead.

News of the raid electrified the nation. Across the country, abolitionists made Brown out to be a martyr. This man was giving his life for the cause of slavery. Northern women wept for him, and Northern newspapers called for other men to follow his example. Poets from the North declared him a saint, and Christian Northerners prayed for his release.

The South was horrified. How could anyone support cold-blooded killing? Did this signal a wide-scale uprising? Southern men and women both began to look at Northerners as people who hated them. Were the Yankees willing to see them assassinated in their beds? Were they ready to support an armed invasion of Southern soil?

By the time Brown was sentenced in court, no one in the South dared speak openly against slavery anymore. Southern legislatures were passing new laws restricting slave travel. Manumission of any kind became illegal. Vigilance patrols on Southern roads and city streets doubled. Traveling salesmen from the North were tarred and feathered and run out of town—just for being from the North!

On December 2, John Brown was hanged. He had already become a legend. Within a year and a half, companies of young volunteers in Union blue would parade down Northern main streets and off to war singing this song:

> John Brown's body lies a-moldering in the grave,
> John Brown's body lies a-moldering in the grave,
> John Brown's body lies a-moldering in the grave,
> His soul goes marching on.

21

THE
VELVET CURTAIN

He will swallow up the . . . veil which is stretched over
all nations. (Isaiah 25:7)

When Congress met in December of 1859, things were not much better. With the entry of Iowa and Minnesota into the Union, the 18 free states now outnumbered the slave states by 3. The balance of power was shifting, and Southerners knew it.

Members of both houses began to arrive at their desks in the Capitol carrying concealed weapons. Civil war was now being spoken of openly by both sides. "We shall welcome you Yankees to bloody graves!" one representative from South Carolina exclaimed. "We will pull the Union to pieces before we submit to be crushed!" vowed a Southern senator.

By February 1860, a man had risen in the Southern ranks to replace Senator Calhoun. Senator Jefferson Davis from Mississippi proposed a national slave code.

"This will guarantee that slaveholders can take their 'property' wherever they like," the tall, brown-haired man in the navy blue long-coat explained. "It will also stop the people of

190

any territory from outlawing slavery until they are actually admitted to statehood." Although Davis did not have enough votes to pass the legislation, this proposal showed just how far the South was now willing to go.

The fuse was about to be lit. The spark that would ignite it would be the Presidential election that fall.

In April of 1860, the Democrats met in Charleston. Within hours, the party had split into fighting factions. Many of the Northerners wanted Stephen A. Douglas to be their Presidential candidate, but the Southern delegates did not trust him and would not be satisfied with any candidate who was not from the South.

This was not the only problem they faced, however. What would be the party's platform? Some delegates wanted to include the slave code.

"Our Northern colleagues ought to be supporting us and declare that slavery is a positive good, not an evil!" one delegate proclaimed.

"We Southerners have come to Charleston to secure our Constitutional rights with a slave code. If we lose, and the doctrine of popular sovereignty is included in the Democratic platform, we'll be bankrupt," Alabama's William L. Yancey warned.

That evening, George Pugh of Ohio rose to reply. "How long must our party be dragged at the chariot wheel of 300,000 slave masters?" he demanded. How could Northern Democrats uphold slavery as right and good? The atmosphere in the room was as chilly as a December day. "Gentlemen of the South," he cried, "you mistake us! *You mistake us! We will not do it!*"

The next morning the leader of the delegation from Alabama gained the Chair's attention. "Mr. Chairman, I have an announcement to make."

He spoke loudly enough for everyone to hear. A hush fell over the assembly as he walked to the front of the hall.

"Our delegation was instructed to withdraw from this convention, if we could not obtain a slave code resolution."

At that, the entire Alabama delegation rose and filed out! No sooner had they left their seats, than the chairman of the Mississippi delegation jumped to his feet.

"Mr. Chairman! The delegation from the honorable State of Mississippi must withdraw."

Within minutes, the same words echoed through the hall as the delegations from Louisiana, South Carolina, Florida, Texas, and Arkansas followed. The party split that many feared—and a few had hoped for—was occurring before their eyes.

Like a velvet curtain ripped to pieces by a pair of giant scissors, the Democratic party would never be repaired. A second Democratic conference in Baltimore voted Douglas as their Presidential candidate. Those who had withdrawn held a separate convention nominating John C. Breckinridge of Kentucky. Another group formed the Constitutional Union party and on May 9 nominated John Bell.

In 1860 four candidates would be running for President. The fourth was someone no one expected.

Meeting in Chicago that spring, the Republican delegates were in for a big surprise. Again, slavery was the key issue.

It was the *only* issue. And the man who had already become the national spokesman against slavery was one of their own: Abraham Lincoln.

Since his defeat in the race for the U.S. Senate seat in 1858, Lincoln had continued traveling and speaking, especially in New England. Wherever he spoke, the subject was always slavery. And the newspapers continued to print many of his speeches word for word.

One time, on a bitter cold night in New York City, some 1,500 people had shown up with scarves wrapped tightly around their necks to hear him.

"The only thing that will satisfy our Southern brethren is for us to stop calling slavery wrong and to join them in calling it right." The country lawyer's high-pitched voice almost cracked as he spoke. "We could do this if we thought slavery was right. But we don't, and we can't."

Lincoln looked out at the educated audience in front of him. He held the vast meeting spellbound.

"There can be no middle ground between right and wrong," he declared. "Let us not be slandered from our duty by false accusations nor frightened by threats. Let us have faith that right makes might, and in that faith, to the end, dare to do our duty as we understand it."

The hall had erupted in cheers and applause. Men waved their hats and women their handkerchiefs.

Now, in Chicago, Lincoln's supporters were working furiously on his behalf. The Democratic party was in shambles, so whomever the Republicans nominated would almost certainly become the next President of the United States. They had to get Lincoln in.

Passing among the delegates in the hall, they made deals and tried to firm up votes. On the first ballot, Senator William Henry Seward from New York was way out in front with 173 votes. To everyone's surprise, Lincoln came in second! While he trailed Seward by more than 70 votes, he was ahead of every other nominee. As the others bowed out of the race, more and more delegates sided with Lincoln.

At one point, Lincoln needed only two more votes for the nomination.

Joseph Medill, the publisher of the Chicago *Tribune,* who had covered the Lincoln-Douglas debates, was sitting next to the Ohio delegation. He knew that Ohio might back its own Senator Samuel Chase for the nomination.

"If you can throw the Ohio delegation to Lincoln," Medill whispered to one of the leading delegates, "Chase can have anything he wants," the powerful publisher promised.

The delegate leaned over to his colleagues and then jumped up on his chair. "Mr. President!" he exclaimed, spreading his arms to gain attention. "I rise to change four votes from Mr. Chase to Mr. Lincoln!"

An instant silence took over the hall as everyone digested the news. Then, all at once, a wild and mighty yell erupted. On the roof a cannon blasted as the delegates made the nomination unanimous. Honest Abe was going to the White House!

Like a race horse out of the gate, the 1860 Presidential campaign took off. From South Carolina to Texas, however, Southern leaders made it very clear that if the Republicans came to power, the slave states would leave the Union.

Douglas believed the South and saw himself as the only candidate with the ability to hold the nation together.

"Yes, I care about popular sovereignty," the heavy-set Democratic nominee announced, "but I care even more about the Union."

Crowds of people thronged to his speeches. "Make no mistake, I want your vote, but I only want the votes of those who wish the Union saved," Douglas said.

"What if Lincoln is elected?" someone asked after one particular speech. "Are the Southern states justified in seceding? And if the South does secede, would you resist her withdrawal?"

Senator Douglas knew his answer would risk the support of any of his remaining loyal Southern Democrats. But he was a patriot at heart.

"It would be my duty to enforce the laws of the United States and to aid the Government in maintaining the supremacy of the laws against all resistance."

By the time of the actual election, the climate was so dangerous in the South that Northern firms called their salesmen home. In New Orleans for instance, a mob roared down Royal Street after a pale stranger. "Hang him! Hang him!" they cried. In the nick of time, someone rescued him. It turned out the man was a traveling salesman selling campaign medals. When packing up his wares, the poor salesman had failed to remove his Lincoln badge. The oversight had nearly cost him his life. As the mob dispersed, an onlooker observed: "Didn't I tell you? Bound to have war. It's already begun." In a sense, it had.

Southern postmasters began stopping all Northern newspapers. And in the Federal Government, those Southern officials in the right positions were shipping arms and munitions to Southern armories.

A Charleston paper issued the call:

The *under*ground railroad will become the *over*ground railroad. Before Mr. Lincoln is installed, the Southern States will dissolve peaceably their Union with the North. Mr. Lincoln and his abolition cohorts will have no South to reign over.

The dark cloud hovering over the country had once been no bigger than a man's hand. Now, on the eve of the election in 1860, it loomed huge and cold, shot through with jagged streaks of lightning. Within a few months, this cloud would blot out the sun.

EPILOGUE

On November 6, 1860, America went to the polls.

In Springfield, Illinois, the day dawned with cannon fire. Some of Lincoln's supporters had brought a couple of old fieldpieces into town and shot them off. The town didn't mind though. This was going to be a great day in their state. One way or another, whether it be Lincoln or Douglas, a son of Illinois was going to the White House today.

Abe sat quietly in the Governor's room in the State House, directly across the street from the courthouse where most of Springfield would vote. He was in good spirits, telling stories to friends and talking with visitors and reporters. In Mobile, Senator Douglas waited for the results, too.

Around 3:00 in the afternoon, Lincoln walked downstairs and across the street to vote. A shout went up, and a crowd quickly gathered. After he had voted, the Presidential nominee returned across the street.

After the polls had closed that evening, he went to the telegraph office. Operators were receiving the early returns. Lincoln was waiting for news about New York. If he took the Empire State, victory was his. The telegraph keys never stopped clicking. Pennsylvania was secure. And Ohio. And Indiana. But still no word from New York.

Shortly after midnight, Lincoln and his party adjourned to a nearby hall. Some ladies of Springfield had prepared a late supper for them. As Lincoln entered, they asked, "How do you do, Mr. President?" Lincoln smiled and sat down.

All of a sudden, a messenger burst in waving a telegram. "You've won! You've won! The Empire State is safe!" he shouted.

Someone started up the campaign song. Lincoln and the Republicans had won.

Down in Mobile, there was no singing or wild cheering. Stephen A. Douglas had learned the results, too. He and his secretary, James Sheridan, quietly walked back to their hotel through the deserted streets. Douglas looked sad. But it was not the election results that were depressing him that night. He could see what was coming. The Union he loved so much was about to be torn in two. There was nothing anyone could do to stop it now. His heart was breaking.

This election became one of the most important elections in the nation's history. Although Lincoln's position was clear, the South could not hear him. He had told them that if elected, he would take no action against slavery where it was already established. But Southerners believed that Lincoln's election meant that war had been declared on slavery, and hence, on them. The states of the Deep South had repeatedly said that if a Republican was elected President, they would secede. The North was not hearing them.

Lincoln believed that the majority of the Southern people did not want to leave the Union even if he was elected. He was right. But in the South, the majority was no longer making the decisions.

After the election, Alexander Stephens of Georgia, wisest of the Southern leaders and a friend of Lincoln's, wrote the new President.

"The country is certainly in great peril," he said, "and no man ever had heavier responsibilities than you have at this present . . . crisis."

"The South is in no more danger than she was in the days of George Washington," Lincoln wrote back. "I suppose though, this does not meet the case. You think slavery is *right* and ought to be extended; while we think it is *wrong* and ought to be restricted. That, I suppose, is the rub."

As 1860 drew to a close, men and women of spiritual vision could see armies of angels and archangels gathering for the coming struggle for the soul of America. They could hear the sound of distant trumpets that would never call retreat. War was close at hand.

Now, as this century closes, men and women of vision are again seeing signs and wonders. These indicate that God's judgment is close at hand. Each of us is familiar with the problems troubling our country: divorce, drug abuse, the murder of unborn children through abortion, children killing children, public officials lying, cheating, and stealing.

It is too late for a human solution. But with God, nothing is impossible. The only hope for America is a national revival. Even now, pockets of genuine spiritual awakening are springing up around our country. But at best America has a case of "revival measles," with spots of spiritual awakening popping up here and there. However, before a revival can spread from coast to coast, more than a few of us will have to take God's promise in 2 Chronicles 7:14 to heart. Each of us, adult and child, must repent, seek His face, and turn from our wicked ways.

And we must do so at once.

At the close of *Uncle Tom's Cabin,* Harriet Beecher Stowe wrote this: "O Church of Christ, read the signs of the times! A day of grace is yet held out to us . . . [for just as surely as a] millstone sinks in the ocean [so surely] injustice and cruelty shall bring on nations the wrath of Almighty God."

The wrath Mrs. Stowe foresaw coming in her time was the terrible tragedy of the Civil War. Heaven only knows what disaster awaits us in our time if we do not, as a nation, turn back to God.

One thing is certain: We can hear the sound of distant trumpets.

GLOSSARY

abolition (n)—the act of ending or abolishing something

abolitionist (n)—a person who wants to end slavery

abyss (n)—a bottomless pit

amphibious (adj)—can work on both land and water

appropriate (v)—to take possession of

arroyo (n)—a gulley carved out by water

ballast (n)—gravel or broken stone

buckeyes (n)—trees of the horse-chestnut family; also a nickname for people who live in Ohio

caisson (n)—a two-wheeled vehicle that carries ammunition

canister (n)—encased shot for close-range artillery

cantle (n)—the back part of a saddle, usually curved upward

censure (v)—to reprimand officially

compromise (n)—an agreement

constituency (n)—the residents of a district who elect a representative

contempt (n)—the act of despising or strongly disliking

debt (n)—something owed

dragoons (n)—armed troops on horses

draymen (n)—men who hauled goods in low, heavy carts without sides emancipation (n)—an act of setting free

emissary (n)—a representative

encampment (n)—the place where troops camp

entreaty (n)—a plea

grapeshot (n)—a cluster of small iron balls shot from a cannon

gringos (n)—a word used by Mexicans to refer to Americans

gristmill (n)—a mill for grinding grain

hoax (n)—a trick

illusion (n)—something that seems real but is not

impending (adj)—near or about to happen

infuriate (v)—to make very angry

jurisdiction (n)—a territory within which authority may be exercised

lead type (n)—metal letters and numbers used in a printing press

loathe (v)—to hate

malignant (adj)—very bad, having an evil influence

maneuver (v)—to perform a specific military movement

manumission (n)—the act of freeing a slave

mule skinners (n)—mule drivers

munitions (n)—material used in war

notorious (adj)—famous, often with a bad reputation

omniscient (adj)—having complete understanding and wisdom

ordeal (n)—a severe, very difficult experience

parliamentary (adj)—pertaining to a legislature

perpetuate (v)—to cause to last indefinitely

phenomenal (adj)—extraordinary

platform (n)—the principles adopted by a political party or candidate

predecessor (n)—someone who previously occupied a position or office

purports (v)—claims to be something, often falsely

radical (adj)—extreme

ravenous (adj)—extremely hungry

reconnoiter (v)—to survey enemy territory

recon patrol (n)—a military troop surveying enemy territory

redoubt (n)—a fortification

redress (n)—relief from a distress

rescind (v)—to repeal

ruffian (n)—a bully

secede (v)—to withdraw membership from an organization

seismic waves (n)—tremors caused by an earthquake

sinister (adj)—evil

Slave Power (n)—the proslavery leadership in the South

stump speaker (n)—a person who travels around making political speeches

tally (n)—a record or count of something

vigilant (adj)—watchful

volatile (adj)—easily aroused

wadding (n)—short, loose fibers used for stuffing into cannons, to hold powder and ball in place

STUDY QUESTIONS

Chapter 1

1. What does the right to petition Congress allow citizens of the United States to do?
2. What was the Pinckney Gag Rule?
3. In 1837 John Quincy Adams was a representative in the United States House of Representatives. What had he done before this?
4. What was JQA trying to protect by opposing the Pinckney Gag Rule?
5. Define the Covenant Way.

Chapter 2

1. List three reasons why emancipating the slaves was difficult for the South.
2. What is an "abolitionist"?
3. Name one famous abolitionist.
4. In 1787, what Congressional act abolished slavery north of the Ohio River?
5. Who started the newspaper called the *Liberator*?
6. What was the difference between Benjamin Lundy's view of freeing the slaves and William Lloyd Garrison's view?

Chapter 3

1. Write three complete sentences about the Lane Debate.
2. Name the most famous Lane Rebel.
3. Why were the Lane Rebels important in our history?

Chapter 4

1. Who was "Old '76"?
2. Name two incidents that hurled John Quincy Adams headlong into the fight against slavery.

Chapter 5

1. Who was Old Rough and Ready?
2. Who was the President of the United States in 1845?
3. (True or False) The Mounted Lancers were American sharpshooters.

Chapter 6

1. Define *Manifest Destiny.* Why was it important in the 1840s?
2. What general won the battle at Vera Cruz?
3. Name a famous captain under this general's command.
4. The War with Mexico had another name. What was it?
5. What secret did President Polk know that others did not?

Chapter 7

1. The First Missouri Mounted Volunteers were a famous regiment. Why?
2. Who was their commander?
3. Name a particular incident when God's hand clearly helped the Volunteers.

Chapter 8

1. How did Robert E. Lee help the American troops?
2. Name the lieutenant who took the Belén Gate. What did he later become?

3. Who became the Mexican dictator during the war between the United States and Mexico?

Chapter 9

1. What happened in California in 1848?
2. Name three reasons people mined for gold.
3. List three things that might happen to a miner.

Chapter 10

1. When did John Quincy Adams die?
2. List five inventions that changed the country during the years between 1830 and 1850.
3. Which invention changed things the most?

Chapter 11

1. Would you have been for or against slavery during the 1840s? Why?
2. What three arguments would you have used to try to convince the other side?
3. List three concerns facing a Southern Congressman in the 1840s. Now list three facing his Northern colleague.

Chapter 12

1. How would you have felt if you had been Elizabeth Keckley?
2. If you had been a Christian slave owner in the South before the Civil War, how would you have treated your slaves? What would you have done if one disobeyed you?

Chapter 13

1. What Southern senator termed slavery "a great good"?

2. Two special men tried to keep the Union together in 1850. Who were they? Did it work?

3. Henry Clay proposed three resolutions. What were they?

Chapter 14

1. What does UGRR stand for?

2. (True or False) Harriet Beecher Stowe worked in the UGRR.

3. What did the book *Uncle Tom's Cabin* do for the abolitionist movement?

4. In your own words, retell the story of William and Ellen Craft.

Chapter 15

1. What was so important about the Territories of Kansas and Nebraska?

2. How did the Missouri Compromise affect these two territories?

3. Who chaired the powerful Committee on Territories? What bill did he get passed?

Chapter 16

1. What incident motivated Lincoln to go into law?

2. (True or False) Abe Lincoln was born in Illinois.

3. (True or False) Lincoln supported the Kansas-Nebraska Act.

Chapter 17

1. Name three events that made 1857 an important year.

2. Who was Dred Scott?

3. What did the Supreme Court say about the Missouri Compromise?

Chapter 18

1. Why were the Fulton Street Meetings famous?
2. Define *revival*.
3. What was different about this wave of the revival?

Chapter 19

1. Where did Abraham Lincoln get the phrase "a house divided"?
2. Who was Lincoln's opponent in the 1858 Congressional race in Illinois?
3. Which man would you have voted for? Why?

Chapter 20

1. Where was Harpers Ferry? What happened there?
2. Do you think John Brown was crazy? Why or why not?
3. How did the South react to the raid?

Chapter 21 and Epilogue

1. The Democratic party split right before the Presidential election of 1860. Why?
2. On what date in November 1860 was Abraham Lincoln elected President?
3. What grieved Senator Douglas more than anything else?